The Kristin Book

by

Robert Nichols

---

and

The Kristin Book: 2013 Update

by

Robert Nichols

with

Carol Nichols and Kristin Nichols

The Kristin Book: 2013 Update
by Robert Nichols

First Printing 1987
Second Printing (e-publishing) 2013

ISBN: 0-930161-12-2
Electronic publishing ISBN: 978-0-9627615-5-3
Paperback ISBN 978-0-9980910-2-0

Illustrated by: Eddie Thomas

1987 edition Published by:
State of the Art, Ltd.
1625 South Broadway
Denver, Colorado 80210
303 722 7177

2013 edition Published by:
Mountain Muse Publishing
P.O. Box 406
Lincoln City, OR 97367
MtMusePublishing.com

Dedicated to:

Hattie Marie Nichols

and

Bernice Marie Riehl

Table of Contents

A note about this update to *The Kristin Book*

March 10, 2013
Coffee House
Newport, Oregon

In the next week or so, Carol, Kristin, and I are going to e-publish this new edition of *The Kristin Book*, inclusive of the original 1987 text (with a few minor corrections) and a new section to bring this work up to date. I just finished rereading my book (the first sixteen years of my daughter's life as a person born with Down syndrome), and I truly hope that the other patrons of this establishment—the texters and web-surfers and, Face-Bookers *et al.*—don't notice that I'm crying.

Or, on second thought, let them witness the honest emotions of a fuzzy-faced old man. It might do their youthful views of this world some good. Hey, maybe someone will lend me a hankie.

The original version of this book took me over ten years to write. I mean, we're not talking *War and Peace* here. With large print and a small format, it barely inked out at a hundred pages. As I strive today to avoid shorting out the keyboard of my laptop with tears, I recall why it was such a long process and, most importantly, why our little story is still relevant over forty years after the birth of Kristin.

Committing the deeply personal truths of a life is a wrenching process of memory, emotion, and soul-felt openness. This was an important story to tell and one that had to be told with a raw edge of honesty that was sometimes hard to face. I had to talk about my Carol's brush with suicide, my Kristin's encounters with a cruel and

1

ignorant world, and my own nearly psychotic avoidance of reality that, for the first year or so, undermined my own usefulness both as a husband and a father.

And if that were all there was to *The Kristin Book,* then it would be a nice little work of limited interest.

But, I believe it is more than a sad and sentimental tale of a small family confronting seemingly impossible obstacles to happiness. Though in places it is sad, and I make no apologies about the role of sentiment in the telling of my truths; the story I tell is one of hope and humor in the face of difficulty. It relates as much today as it did decades ago to the situations all of us encounter in a life fully lived.

This is not a book about Down syndrome, though this chromosomal abnormality is certainly the central issue at its core. Our daughter was born with a terrible stigma attached to her pretty little being. According to the experts who counseled us those early days, she wasn't supposed to amount to much. And, believe me, as her parents we didn't have a clue as to how to give her the life we had imagined for our child. From the day after Kristin's birth, when Carol called me at work from the maternity ward of the hospital and told me, "There's something wrong with our baby," through this morning nearly forty-three years later when Kristin heads out into her world, a lovely lady whose life of grace, good heart and spiritual magic blesses any who have the good fortune to encounter her, this is a tale of love, humor and compassion relevant to the humanity of us all.

Some years ago, I was having a beer at a ragged old high-mountain tavern when, in a roar of a voice, my bear-sized buddy Norm Simmons bellowed at me, "Nichols, I've got a problem with you." My initial reaction, of a sort that has served me well over these years, was to make a run for it out the back door. But I didn't. Norm was a heavy equipment operator, truck driver, and renowned barroom brawler loved and feared by many. I took a chance that my friend wasn't too likely to kill me.

I stepped down to his end of the bar and said, "So, what's up, Norm?"

The large man lithely spun around and stood up. He reached into the pocket of his coat and pulled out a worn copy of *The Kristin Book*. "Hell, Bob," he said as he put a big hand on my shoulder, "your damned book made me cry."

I just grinned. "And...?" I asked.

"...and laugh, and feel a bunch of stuff like that."

Yeah!

The Kristin Book (1987)

Introduction

The power of these words originates in the power of my own rage and sorrow and joy. This book is the product of sincere, poetic perception of a life-deep situation which, at times, has been exceedingly difficult to face.

This is the story of the first sixteen years of my daughter's life and of the influence of those years upon the lives of her parents. It is also a book about compassion and the world.

Kristin is a fine and pretty young lady who, early in the moments of her precious life, was described as being a "non-human," a "vegetable."

Her congenital condition, Down syndrome, is not particularly rare. Kristin Marie Nichols, however, is an extremely rare and truly exceptional human being.

I did not write this book for a limited audience. It was my purpose to communicate to many people. I think my words will benefit parents, teachers, doctors, and especially the mass of us who normally spend our days out on the gawking edges of the whole issue of physical or mental "abnormality."

The Kristin Book is neither maudlin, nor is it bitter. It is intended to be an articulate and honest expression of an important message.

The Beginning

Kristin lost all of her hair when she was three years old. She was beginning to lose her eyebrows too when, perhaps touched by the severity of Their cruelty in the dulling of her face, the Gods relented in this minute way and allowed them to regrow. The Gods had already worked Their dark magic upon her mind and upon every cell of her body. I wrote a poem about it.

The Manila Folder

They had your future in a manila folder labeled "Kristin Nichols."
We saw it on a Denver summer afternoon.
It was deep in the thousand-celled, honeycomb clinic,
where people in white robes work
and people in street clothes wait.
"You see," said the man of medicine
(kind and with eyes deep into the pathos
of helpless knowledge),
"on the twenty-first set there are three chromosomes instead of two."
And we saw the blotches—carefully patterned by nature;
sorted, magnified
and printed by man.
"You see," he said
"all of the pairs and one triplet—
she'll never be
a computer programmer,
or a secretary,
or a lady taxi cab driver."
and then we left, you were so small—
a dozen days or so at most—
and already we knew you'd never like
James Joyce.

She was four months old and I was attempting seclusion in a corner of a teachers' lounge. It was her first autumn and I was just starting to realize how much she was affecting me. (We have known many autumns since then, and the realization is still growing.) A bone-faced, blond-haired lady came over to me and, with practiced smile and tone of voice, leaned into my space and said, "Mr. Nichols, it was God's Will."

"Oh..." I said.

"Yes, and it's wonderful, I'm sure. Sometimes it is not for us to understand His Wonderful Ways," she said, almost in whispered song.

"I understand His ways," I said in an even voice while staring through her joy-dulled eyes and directly into her empty head.

"You really think that you understand Him?" she asked with one of those pious, near smirks so common to those who have deemed themselves the bearers of the only truth.

"Yes," I assured her, "I thoroughly understand Him and His Wonderful Ways."

"Oh, please, Mr. Nichols, enlighten me."

"It's quite simple. Your God is heartless."

That was a long time ago. Long before the afternoons when Kristin would get home from school with tears dried on her cheeks and tell me, for maybe the third time that week, the mean kids had pulled her wig off. A long time before I had laughed at her funny words and cried with her pretty heart. Long ago—and I meant exactly what I had said. I was young and Kristin was just a soft, warm little being who had been terribly abused by fate. I loved her because she was my baby girl. It's years later now and I still love her as my little girl; but, I also love her because she is my friend and companion. I don't think a lot about Him, of Them, or any of the other What-Have-Yous that supposedly create and then piece-by-piece destroy us in Wonderful Ways. I think about her, and when I do, I forget about Causes and rejoice in the effects. I am constantly filled with dichotomous feelings of joy and sorrow and Kristin's very being which, when truly appreciated, mocks and, for the most part, negates the sorrow.

And, still, there is no denying the fact that she got a rotten deal. I haven't begun to get over it; she never will. It would be quite easy to become lost in such obsessions—very easy—were it not for the fact that; with such limitations, such hindrances to human accomplishment; she is yet a wonderful human being. One of the best I've ever known.

Sometimes when the ever-present rage asserts itself within me and I am shaking and whispering the fervent oaths, Kristin places her hand on my shoulder and says, "It's okay, Dad."

And sometimes it really is.

The Crib

I drove seventy miles per hour, ran stoplights, slid around corners, and cursed the seconds, which sped on ahead of me—impossible to catch. We didn't have a lawn. The front yard was dirt and gravel with large cottonwood trees. The little house was white and sat by itself a mile from town, with acres of green alfalfa fields and distant red cliffs surrounding it. The screen door was locked. I knew it would be locked. It was logical she would have locked the screen door. I ripped the door open, leaving the hook dangling from the eyelet screwed into the doorframe. I burst into the living room and saw my wife, Carol, sitting calmly at the kitchen table. The room was silent, except for the tingling of a tiny bell from the bedroom as Kristin pulled the red satin ribbon that moved the tiny hammer and struck the bell, which hung from the railing of her bright red-and-white crib.

Carol was still talking on the telephone to John. I had stopped at John's apartment for a beer and had called her, and then realized that she was probably trying to kill herself. John had known, too, and kept talking to her as I had rushed home. I was in time, but somehow, it seemed so hopeless that I just stood there for a moment staring at the pieces of broken glass lying on the table and the dried, dark trickles of blood staining her pretty arm as she joked with John and avoided looking at me.

We hadn't brought Kristin directly home from the hospital. It is wise not to be embittered by the unintentional malice of the ignorant, but it is difficult to arrive at an objective viewpoint concerning a human life and love. The doctor had said to think about having other children. The doctor had said this child was imperfect and should be institutionalized as soon as it was old enough. The doctor used words like "severely," and "institution," and "it." I think a nurse was the first who used the word "vegetable."

The doctor talked to Carol and said the words that haunted her pretty being for years and whispered death wishes and insanity throughout her conscious and subconscious existence. He said, "Think of *it* as being dead." He said to Carol, and with only the best of misguided intentions, "Think of *it* as being dead... a *non-human*...put *it* in the State Home and have another baby as soon as possible." (Visions of monsters; nightmares of hideous inhuman creatures; a non-human baby borne of her flesh.)

There were friends with awkward good intentions and acquaintances with careful greetings. And from unexpected corners of our world came the closeted parents of children who had been institutionalized or had been taken in by grandparents. Their eyes told us that their hearts were torn when they spoke to us, and yet, they knew it was right for them to speak. Some of them were near strangers; some were longtime friends—people at work, people who barely knew us. Many spoke to us and they all said the same thing: Put her into the State Home.

If we had only been watching them closely. If only we had not been quite so willing to accept their words. If only my mind had not been so ready to run—I would have seen in their faces that they were lying to us and, of course, to themselves.

In Grand Junction, Colorado, there is the State Home and Training School where people like Kristin spend their entire lives under the supervision of underpaid personnel and the watchful eye of closely budgeted care. The doctor had said Kristin should go there. I talked to the people at the Home on the afternoon of Kristin's second day and they told me she would have to be at least two years old before they could take her. The man to whom I spoke recommended that we contact the Department of Social Services to arrange for foster parents until she was old enough to be placed in the institution for the rest of her life.

"Sure," I said.

11

"Carol, they say we probably ought to give Kristin up," I said.

She knew. She had heard the whispers of nurses, seen the eyes of those who avoided her. When she asked her doctor what was wrong with Kristin he had, with all of his well-meaning medicine, turned in silence and left the hospital room.

Already they had given Carol a shot which prevented her breasts from producing milk.

* * * *

Carol stayed up all night making curtains for our old Dodge station wagon. I went to Grand Mattress the next day and bought a large piece of scrap foam. It was July. Kristin was a month old and living with foster parents across the valley from the white house and us. We were getting out of town in an attempt to make everything feel better. We would stay at campgrounds and sleep in the car. It would be just as it had been for the previous four and a half years of our marriage. We rafted on the Green River in Utah; we canoed on the Flaming Gorge Reservoir in Wyoming; we camped by Bear Lake in Idaho; we wandered through the International Food Bazaar in Seattle and rode to the top of the Space Needle; we rented a one-room cabin on the Olympic Peninsula where the Pacific Ocean ceaselessly explodes upon the rocky shoreline, and where eerie inland valleys are ever grey and pale-green in rain forest mist.

"I can't sleep with the light on," I had said as we lay in the back of the station wagon on the foam mattress with the curtains pulled shut. It was the first night of the trip and she had our six-volt lantern burning.

"I can't be in the dark," she said.

Later by the ocean in a seven-dollar cabin with the one light hanging from a wire in the middle of the room burning all night as we continued a week-long rummy game into the tens of thousands of points. Of course, we knew something was terribly wrong. We never spoke of Kristin.

I seldom consciously thought of her; Carol seldom thought of anything else.

A few weeks were expended and we returned home. I was a teacher and still had another month before I had to go back to work. My parents came from Virginia to visit us. We sat out under the huge cottonwood trees in the front yard at night watching for falling stars and drinking beer. One afternoon, Carol and I went to the foster home and picked up Kristin so her grandparents could see her and hold her for a while. We still have pictures of that afternoon and our faces are tight with sorrow and loss. My father's gentle, honest eyes speaking from within the stoic exterior of his strong being. My mother's magical, loving hands; the glow of her glad face; the inference of her life-long heart upon the moment of the visiting granddaughter.

I took Carol to a dentist the last week of August. She went into the office while I stretched out on the foam pad which we had left in the back of the car and drifted off to sleep. Sometime later, I was startled by frantic tapping on the window. A lady from the dentist's office told me that something was wrong with my wife. I found her in a semi-conscious state, lying in the reclined dental chair, muttering the name of our child.

We still laugh about how ridiculous it was for an intelligent, well-educated participant in the Twentieth Century to hyperventilate while having a tooth filled. The unfortunate dentist had been in practice for only a few weeks at the time and seemed to be on the verge of taking in a little extra oxygen himself.

It's strange what things can become the catalysts of truth. If Carol hadn't had a toothache, it's hard to speculate about how long we would have continued the farce of our separation from Kristin. Sometimes I think about myself and what an empty life I would have had if it were not for Carol's toothache, Carol's heartache, Carol's honesty. If it weren't for her obsession that kept us up nights with lights burning and cards shuffling, and that finally put her into dental-hysteria; I could have spent my whole life apart from my child—and also apart from my own truth.

There are so many mistakes to be made in a lifetime. Fortunately, some can be rectified.

The next day we began repurchasing baby equipment and made arrangements for bringing Kristin home. We stayed up all night painting the used crib I had found at Goodwill—neither of us could sleep.

The Years

It's been a long time since we painted that red-and-white crib and made a permanent space in our lives for Kristin. A very long time. I've been trying to write this for ten years and have only produced six pages. At this rate, I'll be long dead before I've even begun to tell anything.

It's just that it has been so hard to deal with parts of it. I call myself a poet, yet, I haven't felt that I've had enough power in my words or self to express either the rage or the joy of it all. Perhaps I never will—but I'd better give it a try. Kristin has been on my case about writing "the Kristin book" for years now. She's old enough to know what a story it is herself. I guess if she can face this, I should be able to at least attempt it.

You see, it still hurts. Even when it feels the best, when her being transcends her syndrome, when my pleasure and pride in her nearly extinguish my sorrow—it still hurts.

These years have been full of wonder and miles and near-suicide and insanity. They've been full of time and my whiskers are half white and my face is sometimes the face of a man ten years my senior. They have been full of laughter and hysteria; rage and love. These years.

I'm not complaining. They've been full of the stuff of a poet.

I'll show you.

John

Kristin was fifteen months old when John Gleason stopped over for a beer after work one day and ended up sleeping on our living room couch for the better part of the next nine months. He was a crazy Irishman full of bullshit and hope. He could spout theories of life and death and reincarnation and magic that would simultaneously fill you with profound wonder, and with the mirth of the ridiculous. One could never completely believe that John was real, and yet, never doubt that his plethora of manifestations was as real as feeling and compassion can be.

His talking and his blarney and his laughter and, mostly, his honest belief in Kristin (a fellow Gemini) combined into a spell of comfort-crazed distraction that saved Carol's life. Perhaps mine as well.

It was a September full moon and John and I were sitting out in the front yard on the tailgate of my old station wagon, and nothing was hurting very much. It was a little bit cold but we were a little bit drunk and the moon made the night sharp and clear. Carol came out with a glass of wine in her hand and we were laughing. It was easy to breathe.

In those days it wasn't always easy to breathe or to know there was any certain route that would get us all to the next tomorrow. I'll never try to analyze it. It probably had something to do with whatever biological, sociological, or personal demands and expectations swim the aura of motherhood. It doesn't matter. Somewhere in every day there was insanity.

(Kristin's crib was in a corner of the bedroom next to the curtain that divided it from the living room. We would put her to bed and then sit on the red Mediterranean couch

16

and wait for the edge of the curtain to move and for her to peek at us and giggle. It was a wonderful game.

Her first pseudo-word was "lur" and we would talk to her in the language of "lur" and listen to her as we began to know her humor and her love and her wisdom. And for a long time she would wake us up at exactly 6:16 a.m. with a little squeak. I can remember lying there smiling at the sound of the squeak. Carol and I listening to the squeak of our waking child and smiling our first morning moment of the day.)

It wasn't all crazy. Most of it was love. It's just that it was seldom, if ever, completely safe from being crazy.

Carol's depression, my avoidance: insanity. Tingling bells, dripping blood, and me wandering around like a porcelain poet assuring my world, my wife, and myself that nothing was wrong.

You see, women don't just have abnormal babies and shrug it off as a little chromosomal mishap. Women build babies out of themselves. Men shoot their pleasure and then pamper and buy ice cream and go to breathing classes and pelvic-rock classes. Men proudly pat swelling abdomens and learn to make love in awkward, giggling ways, and listen with their grinning faces against the fetal impatience of their impending progeny. Women go to work every morning (except when they throw up too long) and they come home and all day their lungs fill with air and their blood fills with oxygen and they swell up and their bodies build babies from themselves.

And Kristin had an extra chromosome and Carol had an irrational and unbearable sense of guilt. Never in all the distraught distortions of her reality did she resent the child she had borne: but, seldom in those times did she forgive herself for the misfortune of Kristin's complications.

* * * *

17

So John and Carol and I had some more beer and wine and everything was all right in the September full-moon world for a while.

We laughed in the early autumn night and John told us about the moon and magic and it wasn't frightening because he knew not to tell about the devils and their demons.

John was tall and wore wire-rimmed glasses and even though he had an apartment in town he usually slept on our red Mediterranean couch and it was good when he stayed.

It helped us both breathe.

It had been months with Carol's wide-opened eyes in the middle of the night—eyes darting about the room avoiding the head-on stares of ghastly apparitions of her own distorted truth. Months of awaking to the tremble of our bed as she shook with silent tears. It had been months with my distortion of reality—considerably less overt, but equally imperceptive. Months of everything being just fine and me just waiting around for tomorrow to become possible out of the impossibility of each night.

And then, the night of the tailgate and the moon and Carol's smiling wine, John set aside his laughter and his mystical malarkey, and wept against the cruelty of the forces he so honestly tried to understand. Something happened. Something cut loose inside of me, and in my own open and visible sorrow it all seemed to have headed back up a long and arduous, often nightmarish and torturous path towards a bearable and bitterly beautiful truth for all of us. What might have begun that night took years to complete, but something did begin the night of the beer and the visible honesty.

Carol had decided to go to bed and she was smiling and I thought that she would be all right. John and I went down the road to a bar where the people spoke Spanish and the Friday night beer was perfect for talking too much or, perhaps in this case, just beginning to talk.

I told John about the best and worst times of my life.

18

Kristin was born at 11:33 one Sunday morning in June at St. Mary's Hospital in Grand Junction, Colorado. I was there because we had read books and practiced breathing and pushing together for months. I was ready to be there. The delivery room was cruel and cold and dominated by stainless steel, and Carol was warm and alive and hurting so much when the contractions came. She was pretty and strong and scared and I loved her and panted with her like a dog pants to help with her "D" level pressure. "Pressure, hell," she would say during the respites of ebbing contractions, "this hurts." And I was so proud of her the way she was pushing our baby out all by herself. I was holding her hand and talking about funny things from behind my clown-suit robe and surgical mask. I remembered the things to say about pushing and breathing and I held her hand, but she was all alone with the baby that she had built out of herself.

And she pushed Kristin right out into the world. I stood by the doctor and saw the wet curl of hair on the top of her head as she began to emerge. I watched and Carol pushed and then, in marvelous dust-blue dampness, there was Kristin. It seemed like the best moment in my life.

The beer was working and there was much beer as the Mexican band played and the crowd grew warm and drunk. John listened to me and he knew what I was telling him about that June morning of Kristin's birth. And he knew that the two of them were Geminis and knew things that only Geminis could know. He would talk to her when she was only fifteen months old but she would listen and sometimes she would say "lur" and sometimes she would use her little words that were definitely coming, but usually she would just grin and listen.

And I told him the worst time.

It happened at the school where I worked. It was the day after Kristin was born. I could have stayed off another day or so but I was eager to get back to work so that I could strut around like new fathers get to do. I was so happy that, when I would tell people, they would have to smile for my happiness.

19

There was a phone call for me. It was after lunch and I was smiling and teaching English to a class of eighth-graders, and even they were smiling beyond their normal affectation of apathy. A teacher covered my class and I went to the phone. It was Carol and I could hear the fear and sadness in her voice—the terror. She said she knew that something was wrong with our baby. The nurses were avoiding her and when she asked her doctor what was wrong he had turned and walked out of the room without speaking. "There's something wrong with our baby," she said.

I can still almost feel the way I did that day. The earth was falling out from under me as I told the teacher who I had quickly enlisted to cover my class, "I've got to go. There's something wrong with my baby."

I guess the music must have been really loud in the bar, and I knew that I had said things that were not easy to repeat. I had been talking to my friend but mainly I was talking to myself and it was a short while after I finished telling the bad times before I noticed that my big Wyoming buddy, John, had tears in his eyes and on his face. He made no effort to hide his feelings. He looked right at me and then smiled and said, "She's a beautiful kid, Bob."

I nodded because I knew he was right.

"And damned if she isn't a Gemini, too!" he said.

And I was grinning that night of Mexican music and Budweiser beer. Grinning after I had just told the worst time of my life.

* * * *

I'll tell the rest of that night because where it ends is really where so much begins. We left the highway bar and went to a place downtown where people drank cocktails and the beer cost fifty cents more a bottle and something was beginning to fly right out of me. I came out of the men's room and told John that we'd better leave because I had just destroyed the towel machine. I had crushed the damn thing, and it would probably be a good thing for us to leave because for the first time in my life I really felt like crushing things. We were laughing, of course, and when we got to the car I punched the windshield and made it look like a giant spider web. We laughed and drove thirty miles out into the desert where the moon was far to the west and the stars were huge in the black sky. We drove a hundred miles per hour back to town and I dropped John off at his place and headed back to mine.

She was awake when I got home and that worried me when I saw the lights and was afraid that she might be in trouble. But she was sane and it didn't take her but a moment to see that I was not.

The last time I had cried as a kid I was nine years old and my father had spanked me for being a smart ass, and then I hadn't cried again until the evening of Kristin's second day when I had called my parents to tell them about her being mentally retarded. My father had been unable to speak for a few seconds before saying sorry and to give Carol their love and then good-bye. Carol was standing by me in a robe in the hall of the hospital with a hand on my waist and her head against my shoulder. We walked to the room where fathers waited for their children to be born. There was nobody there. I sat down on the arm of a couch and pressed my face against her empty abdomen and cried.

It was very late on the night of the moon and the laughter and the broken windshield and I was curled up on the couch with my head upon her lap and she was holding me and I was sobbing for all the injustice of it, and for all the rage of it, and for all the times I should have cried since I had been nine.

She was holding me and I was crying. Finally, after all of those months of comforting her grief and ignoring my own, I was showing her my sorrow, my rage, my tears.

Carol is a strong person. She was strong even then when, at times, survival was questionable. I had spent so long trying to protect her from an agony that I couldn't even confront. It's taken me half a lifetime to know this, but sometimes sheltering loved ones is the worst thing you can do for them or for yourself. Something changed that night of the unleashed sorrow. It had surprised us both. It might have been the beginning of the most intense flurries of insanity. The things that flew out of me that night of long suppressed weeping and honesty were ancient things and wildly bitter. But, I believe that it was the beginning of health for both of us, though it would be years before we could realize it.

John Gleason didn't live long enough to know the extent of what he had done for us over those early months, or to see his little Gemini friend become a Gemini young lady. Cancer dropped him down to a hulking skeleton, and then to a memory several years ago when he was still just a kid in his mid-thirties.

But, I can't believe that beer-drinking, Irish Geminis disappear quite so thoroughly as medicine and mortality would claim.

It just seems that Kristin still has a friend out there somewhere; I think all three of us do.

Old Business

There was a poem.

A simple, free verse charting of welcome: Written expectation early in the waiting months, when babies were yet philosophy.

During the turmoil and near-tragic misdirection of Kristin's first days, I quietly retrieved her birth announcement poem from the printer and filed it away in a distant stack of papers in a distant closet. I knew the pain it would evoke.

Another mistake, or just an extension of the same mistake. Kristin did not receive the honor of a formal proclamation of her birth. We were deprived the joy of the flourish of her welcome into our lives and into the lives of our friends and relatives.

There sometimes is kindness in silence and survival in avoidance; but, there is also loss.

Carol eventually exhumed the announcement and gave it a place in the Baby Book. It is there now—roughly typed and with the printer's notes about color and print size jotted along its margins.

Seventeen years late; but, why not?

Poems are supposed to last forever.

Kristin Marie Nichols

Born on
June 7, 1970

to

Robert and Carol Nichols

To Kristin

We welcome you, child.
We shall hold you and watch your
squirming life take form,
we'll walk with you—tasting and
feeling worlds with you.
We will teach you our songs.
We'll show you all of the joy and beauty
that we can share.
We will build for you a place in our love.

And hope,
through all of the distances and times
you will see and know,
that we can fulfill our portion
of your needs.

Your Parents

'tink

Let me tell you about Kristin's early years. It was good to be there; it was good to watch her grow and learn and become the nicest kid I've ever known. I'll tell you about some people who helped her and about some bastards who almost killed her.

When she was eighteen months old we took her to the Kennedy Birth Defect Center in Denver for an evaluation of her development and potential. We carried her around to various stations where her physical and intellectual capacities were poked and rolled and noted on graphs and forms.

When she was nine days old we had taken her to the same place for documentation of the diagnosis that she had Down syndrome. They took tissue samples from each of us and at a later date showed us pictures of our chromosomes that proved our hometown physicians were correct. Kristin had an extra chromosome—her twenty-first pair was a triplet. Still is.

Dr. Arthur Robinson, who did the analysis, was a good man who had compiled data from thousands of cases of Down syndrome. The conversation he had with Carol and me, he must have had with countless others in the same despairing moments of their lives. He listened to our questions. When he answered them and when he asked us his questions, we didn't feel as though we were part of some cold scientific investigation. He was a nice man who was trying to find the answer to a terrible question. Our chromosomes were normal, and the chromosomes of our aunts and uncles and parents and grandparents had apparently been equally well-matched sets of Celtic-English/German normalcy. Generations of coal miners and farmers and feuding mountaineers and now Kristin.

25

Our chromosomes were fine and we asked why Kristin's were different.

Dr. Robinson was a kind and intelligent man who was looking for the answer to our question and to the same question asked by thousands of distraught, guilt-touched, fate-struck parents of all racial, ethnic, and philosophical backgrounds. He didn't have an answer in 1971, and, to my knowledge, a definitive answer has yet to be found. I know that good people like him are still seeking a key to whatever correlation of diverse variables will explain the presence of the extra chromosome. Perhaps their answer will be discovered soon. I hope so. I don't think about it very much.

At eighteen months, Kristin giggled when they poked her and we were so proud when she spoke her words, and when she made her careful way around the edges of tables. We thought she was amazing. She had learned so much.

At the end of the day we met with several members of the staff to discuss the results of the evaluation. We tried not to be too discouraged by what we heard. She might be toilet trained by the time she was six, she might even take her first unaided steps within another six to eight months, as an adult she would probably have a vocabulary of about four hundred words. She was sleeping on my lap while we heard the clinical reading of her future. "She is an average Mongoloid child," the man in the white frock said.

Neither of us said it, but, we both had expected them to tell us that we were raising the most fantastic Down's kid in history. We didn't say much about the evaluation. As we left the medical center and headed back over the mountains toward home, Carol started making a list of all the words in Kristin's vocabulary.

As I said, Kristin was napping during the meeting with the white-frocked prophets. A week after we returned from Denver she walked across the living room by herself.

* * * *

26

I'll write about Hugh next. He's a kind of rugged Cheyenne, Wyoming, guy with a half-bald head that turns red whenever he gets mad and he has a gleam in his eyes that is full of Wyoming rowdy and poet sensitivity. He's a trumpet player and guitar picker who taught band at my school when Kristin was heading toward her second birthday. Hugh would come out to the house we were renting and drink beer and tell funny stories. Sometimes we would go out in the backyard and try to make his orange Karmann Ghia run better. Some of our friends weren't very comfortable around kids and tended to keep their distance from Kristin. We knew their actions were not discriminatory toward our daughter—they steered clear of all babies. Hugh was a major exception to this attitude. When he arrived he would grab hold of Kristin and throw her around and set her on his lap and sing dirty old cowboy songs and sailor songs to her.

There is a serious misconception about children with Down syndrome that they love everybody and are not discerning in the show of their affection. It's not true. From very early in her life, Kristin judged visitors to our home carefully. Sometimes her reactions to people were more accurate than our own. She could sense insincerity from clear across the room.

(And she also has always been intelligent enough to carry a grudge. Our friends Bob and Judy came over for dinner once when Kristin was about fourteen months old. She crawled over to Bob's chair, pulled herself up to a standing position, and smiled at him. Bob gave her a piece of lettuce from his salad that had vinegar and oil on it. Kristin put it in her mouth, tasted it, frowned, cried, and refused to have anything to do with Bob for over a year. She has been very sensitive and selective about people her whole life.)

She loved it when Hugh would come and rough her up and make her laugh. She and Hugh were sitting on the living room floor one Sunday afternoon playing with a red-and-blue ball that had holes cut into it in various geometric shapes. The object was to fit plastic pieces into the holes.

27

Someone had given her the ball and we thought it was nice because it made rattling noises for her when it rolled around the floor. Hugh had higher expectations.

"Goddamn it, kid." We heard him growl, "the egg-shaped piece goes in the egg-shaped hole!"

Later that day Hugh taught her to flip me off, and he was flat on his back laughing like a madman as Kristin grinned and raised her middle finger, and then she sat down in front of her ball and put the egg-shape in the egg-shaped hole and the square-shape in the square-shaped hole.

"She can do it!" Carol yelled.

"Well, hell yeah, she can do it," Hugh said, amazed at our disbelief. "What'd you expect?"

Damn little, I guess.

We expected what they had told us to expect, and we were being very cautious in accepting our realization that "they"—all the white-smocked medical experts, the time-blinded parental experts, and ourselves as experts on pessimism based upon our fears—were wrong.

Kristin Marie Nichols was not, is not, the child of a syndrome.

She is the child of Robert and Carol, conceived in a blissful and loving sexual encounter on some bed-warmed autumn night. A child of the human species, a child of a June morning in 1970. I don't know who Down was or is. I know he named the malady that stole some of my child's intelligence. But, I also know Mr. Down was not the father of my child. She is not a Down's kid; she's a Nichols' kid.

Somewhere between the agonizing deception of denying a limitation's existence and the devastating limitation of the perception of little or no hope, there is a realistic seedbed for the maximum development of human beings. All human beings. Even little girls with extra chromosomes.

We knew she was wonderful, but we had been afraid to believe that she could flip the "bird' or put egg-shaped pieces into egg-shaped holes. Authorities had given us so little to expect from her, and also, we were probably afraid of expecting too much for fear of diminishing our appreciation of what she could do.

We had "syndromed" our own child.

"Just what the hell did you expect?" Hugh had said.

* * * *

And Bob.

There was a time of many friends and Friday night parties and good loud music. Cars would be scattered about the front yard beneath the myriad stars of the clear Colorado sky. Janis Joplin had not been dead for very long.

Once, during one of those early spring nights, Bob and Kristin took the first of countless imagined voyages across mountains and prairies, oceans and galaxies.

Bob, the motorcycle man with motorcycle arms; Bob, the surreptitious stalker of defaulted automobiles; and, Kristin, the dinky little kid, walked outside. Kristin and her buddy, Bob the repo-man, headed out together to clear themselves a moment from the sound and clutter of a fine party. Time passed and, when Carol and I went outside with a friend who was departing our spirited gathering, we heard the familiar sound of the unfettered laughter of our child. It was coming from one of the ugliest cars in America which was parked just beyond the edge of light— facing the expanse of a dark open field and its connected sky. A disjointed compilation of random body parts in rainbow array, aimed arrow-straight at all the universe.

We stood in the shadows near the car just in time to hear Kristin return her spacecraft from Pluto and head her jeep up the Alcan Highway for the slopes of Denali.

"Look out for that moose!" shouted Bob.

The veldt of Africa, the glistening Antarctic ice, the spiraling wonder of the deep night sky. For years my gentle friend Bob has ridden shotgun and navigator through the billion miles of Kristin's dreams.

(For her ninth birthday, he showed up in a block-long Lincoln Continental limousine—a big black monster of an elegant automobile, that he had freshly stolen from the

29

misspent use of a foundered debtor. What moments we all had riding around Greeley like oil people or drug dealers in black-glassed anonymity with Kristin feeling so very special. When we arrived with great flourish at Rich and Betty Rangel's house for her second annual taco, Budweiser, ornate cake and ice cream birthday party, she felt like a movie star.

* * * *

I don't hate very much. I don't hate the Russians. I don't hate the IRS. I don't hate the Gods. But, I certainly felt, and perhaps still feel, hatred for a throat specialist who almost killed my kid. I hate him and the legion of Adolph Hitler, reptilian types that he represents.

Her pediatrician was only incompetent, or ignorant or maybe just over-worked. I never quite figured out what his problem was, but I don't believe he was guilty of any cognizant malice in the treatment of my daughter. He was only stupid; I don't think he was cruel.

In my mind, the throat guy was damned near a murderer.

Kristin was three years old and becoming more and more active and involved in a world that fascinated her. Her health seemed good, except that she had had chronic respiratory problems and was encountering breathing difficulties in her sleep. Many mornings we would find her sitting upright on the floor next to her bed with her head tilted back in an effort to gasp air. There were bruises on her head where she had hit it against the bed frame. We took her to her doctor, but he seemed unable to come up with any definite notion of what was choking the sleep out of her nights.

We got rid of the best dog in America because the doctor thought Kristin's condition could have been caused by an allergic reaction to dog hair. Autumnal Equinox Nichols, Auty, shipped downriver to a friend's house far away because a genuine, state-certified, AMA-approved

30

child-healer couldn't look down a throat and see a goddamn set of swollen tonsils.

Human perception is amazingly inconsistent.

The pediatrician was only worthless; the specialist was a malicious bastard.

We were sent to him because we needed the opinion of an expert on throats.

What we received, and not very subtly, was an opinion that our daughter wasn't worth treating.   This is all extremely subjective. It is difficult at times to discern what is imprecisely construed as a result of bitterness or defensiveness. Sometimes the whole world is staring at your baby and sometimes there is no place, no single person to target with your rage; no definable battle to wage.   There are times when ambient consciousness strikes like a vicious, vindictive thing. Maybe he was just an apathetic son of a bitch. Who knows? Maybe he was thinking about golf, stock market portfolios, or some other such medical priority.

Or maybe, and this is the most insidious possibility (I'll not mention his name because he could probably sue me for looking into his heart and writing what I saw), maybe he didn't think the swollen tonsils in the throat of "a retard" were worth his attention.

Maybe.

He said her tonsils might be bad but there was no reason to remove them—they'd probably grow back anyway. (I wonder if he believes in making beds in the morning.) What he "said" was that he didn't give a damn.

Some nights I would sit up with her in a reclining chair in the living room. Long nights into morning light letting her sleep sitting up in my lap where it was safe and she would not bang her head on the bed frame. Hellishly long nights spent thinking of "apathy" and incompetence and helplessness. The pediatrician mumbled something about "perhaps an allergist"; after he momentarily considered the worthless advice of the specialist. And Kristin and Carol and I continued to witness the dilution of darkness by the steel light of countless dawns through breath-desperate hours.

It was two more doctors, a move, and a year later before a man in Greeley noticed her tonsils were so enlarged that, as he put it, "You couldn't get a pencil down her throat," and went ahead and did the belated surgery.

If it had only been a matter of Kristin's suffering and our frustration (not to mention loss of sleep), the whole development could be filed away in an ever-thickening file of events labeled "Documentation of Gross Incompetence/ Discrimination in the Medical, Social, Educational Life of a Disabled Human Being," and eventually removed from the realm of consciously perceived aggravation.

But it wasn't that simple. It wasn't just the mistreatment of my child by three doctors for a period of over a year. It wasn't just a common childhood malady given intolerable duration by the blindness or possibly genocidal ignorance of a few highly paid incompetents. All that gasping, all those months of contorting her tiny frame in pursuit of breath. The blood about her tonsils was black. Her heart had been seriously damaged. She became listless, bloated; her lips were blue. She was dying.

It was a conference room at Children's Hospital in Denver. It was my shift. Carol was out walking in the park somewhere away from the oppressive smell of disinfectant, the sound of shuffling nurse sneakers, the sound of crying children, the sadness of Kristin's pale face. She was taking her few hours' break in a park when the heart man took me into the conference room and drew the diagrams on a chalkboard and talked about limited life expectancy.

You see, all of that anguished breathing had enlarged part of her heart, and the resulting imbalance had caused much of her blood to bypass the lung part of circulation and its life-giving oxygen.

She wasn't supposed to get well.

But then, she wasn't supposed to piss in a pot until she was six, and she mastered that critical social skill years ahead of schedule.

She wasn't supposed to have more than four hundred words with which to speak all of her truths; and now is seems sometimes that she rattles off at least four hundred a minute when she discusses the importance of rock and roll, the physical and spiritual attributes of Harrison Ford and Bruce Springsteen, or the atrocities committed by her new (non-allergenic) dog, Willie (as in Nelson).

I'd better tell it all. The same pediatrician who overlooked her enlarged tonsils, months earlier saved her from pneumonia. Her right lung had collapsed, she was in an oxygen tent, she was a tiny body in the terror of the harsh and alien environment of a pediatric ward of the local hospital; and he was there with his wonder drugs and his words and his knowledge. He was there, and without him or another like him, she probably would have died back when she was two and a half—long before the bastards had a chance at her heart.

Of course, I'm bitter, lacking in objectivity or sufficient knowledge to judge the situation. Nichols is no doctor— what the hell does he know about hearts and lungs and the complex plumbing of the human body? Just an over-emotional parent striking out at a convenient target, when, in truth, he boxes with the devils of fate which are, as shadows, ever present, ever elusive.

Perhaps.

She wasn't supposed to get well, but she did. Two or three years of daily doses of a modern formulation of an ancient drug called digitalis and she was just about normal. Her heart works, her mind works, her smile and her eyes work. She is yet alive.

* * * *

There were friends and fools and the amazing powers of the human spirit in all their darkness and light. And there was Kristin, alive and watching the whole process.

It was in forest darkness, pulled into a campsite near Mt. Rushmore in South Dakota. It was a cool summer night with sounds of nocturnal things moving and singing their natural ways through the close surrounding trees. My

beat-up old Ford van was home to the three of us—
wearied travelers huddled beside a day's long highway.

I swear, I thought that they were asleep.

I really did.

Beans and their swelling energies, a dark place with three slumbering forms beneath blankets, foam pads for mattresses—quiet save the distant owl sounds, and the rustling rodent sounds, and my whispering gas sounds.

And her tiny voice, the utterance of four-year-old indignation against a night that could only listen, spoke shattering truth to the precipitous silence: "tink," she said.

Education

She loved to swing. Once we were on a picnic at the end of a school year when she was in a trainable class (a basic level of special education) at a local community center in Greeley, Colorado. Her teacher was a beautiful young lady named Kim, and the director of the center was Dr. John Wooster. Kristin loved those days. She was smart and the teachers liked her. It was the beginning of her formal education. She had started there one summer while Carol began work on her doctorate degree at the University of Northern Colorado. It was the first official encounter we had with an encouraging group of professionals. Kristin was three years old and John Wooster told us that she was amazing. He told us what we had known, and yet, had been cautiously reluctant to believe. He told us Kristin was bright and pretty and he was glad to have the opportunity to work with her.

She spent her summer days with the nice people, and we began to realize that the dismal future foretold by so many was only a painful myth.

A year and a half after that summer we moved to Greeley and enrolled Kristin for more learning and succeeding and proving how smart she was.

It was at the end of the school year in early June and we were at a local park with a table of happy kids with Kool-Aid mouths and cake crumbs in the afternoon sun. Paul was autistic, Missy couldn't walk, Annie drooled a humming sound and behind each child one of us parents or teachers or aides was guiding the hilarity of the food and the park and the new summer's day. We moved to the playground and merry-go-round with sticky kids shrieking and spinning joy of that moment's life. Then it was the swings.

35

I wrote a short story about this years ago. Paul disappeared when all of us forgot for a second that the world was a dangerous place, and only sang with the children in the rhythm of the swinging swings and diverted our attention from his tormented isolation. Only a second and he was gone.

His mother was so pretty and so very tired.

My story was about how the surface level of love can appear apathetic when it has been battered by impossibility, and about relativity and ignorance.

It was a good story, I think. Perhaps a bit heavy. No magazine bought it.

It was about a wire-taut child clasping to the rough bark of the high limbs of a tree. A child in a world with no exits.

In reality, we found Paul. I pried his small hands free and returned him to his mother.

The story, my work of fiction, didn't have a happy ending either. It just ended as ensconced in impossibility as it had begun.

An afternoon picnic in the park, a lost child, a found child.

Kristin could swing herself. She could pump with her legs and she would arch her back and swing higher and higher. It might not seem like much to the parents of gifted children whose gymnastic antics are so beautiful to watch. But, oh, how my little girl could swing.

Feet flying in the air, head back with a smile to the sky, joyfully describing higher and higher arcs.

And Paul's mother with time-thickened arms surrounding, entrapping her wire-taut son, looked at the frail children, the misshapen children, the fate-victimized children. She looked at Kristin and said, "What an amazing child. Just look at her swing."

Dr. Wooster and his people saw a promise in Kristin that others had failed to recognize. Even Carol and I. He was right back then when she was a three-year-old little girl with a pretty smile and easy laugh. Those people that summer in Greeley began the formal process of learning which has subsequently covered vast distances.

Kristin's education has taken place in several different locations on three different levels. She began in a trainable class where life skills were taught, then went to an educable class where basic academic skills were taught, and currently spends part of her day in classes that are modified versions of a standard school curriculum.

Generally, she has had good experiences at schools and has maintained a high level of interest in learning. In my years of teaching children in secondary schools, I have seldom encountered individuals with as much enthusiasm for learning as Kristin. I can't tell you the secret of the emergence and maintenance of her attitude. She has known some nice teachers, she has learned much, she has good friends. Perhaps the fact that she is with people of similar mental and physical ability when she is in school is a major factor. Though Carol and I are her blood progenitors and have accompanied her through most of the days of her life, we still are not "one" with her. I suppose that is true of all parents and children on one level or another, but in Kristin's case it's probably a more pronounced difference. Schools have given her a much-needed society.

It started in her brightly-colored baby crib and on the kitchen table and out in the dirt and gravel of the front yard. Carol taught Kristin; I watched and laughed and encouraged. I crawled on my belly next to her creeper; Carol was a master of picture cutouts and ribbon strings. When we had people over, she would put Kristin in her yellow plastic baby holder with the tiny seat belt, and set her right in the middle of the kitchen table so she could listen to the talk and the laughter and see the eyes of talkers and know the rhythm of communication. She had a pair of yellow booties that her grandmother in St. Louis had knitted for her. I can still so clearly picture Carol and John or Judy, Bob, Ken, Hugh, Maelynne—friends long scattered, or gone, diluted by distance and time—and Kristin right in the middle with her yellow booties bobbing up and down as she listened to the songs of that ancient table.

Grandmother Riehl and her prolific knitting needles and her prolific heart turned out seasons of sweaters and hats and mittens. Seasons of wool twisted and knotted into garments of love, ever increasing in dimension. And Kristin learned how to propel her amazing four-wheel-walker when Carol put her out in the driveway gravel that tickled her bare feet and caused her to push and roll. There were thick cardboard pictures hanging from red ribbons in her crib, and one day she started turning them around so that she could see the pictures on the other side. She always looked at magazines right side up. There were always music and books and things that rattled and things that rang. There were actions, reactions, big round balls. There were always hands to touch her, words to encourage her. She flourished in an atmosphere of stimulation and love.

She began her first regular school year when she was four. We enrolled her in a deluxe and renowned school in Boulder where her teacher was really impressed with the fact that she could blow her own nose. One autumn day we were getting ready to go out and, instead of putting her coat on by sliding her arms into the sleeves in the normal manner she had used for some time, she laid it out in front of her and then flung it over her head while inserting her arms into the sleeves. "Where'd you learn how to do that?" I asked.

"School," she said.

And we realized early in her career as a student that even at deluxe, renowned schools, teaching has to be monitored if the needs of an individual are to be accurately met. The "over the head" technique is used to help children who lack sufficient coordination to master more conventional means of putting on their coats. Kristin was being taught to regress.

Some of the problems Kristin has encountered in her education are significant beyond the scope of children requiring special education. We all have to be very careful with the learning process.   It should be treated as a systematic approach to teaching a finely tuned progression of skills leading to the utmost level of survival possible for an individual.   Sometimes in the swampy seas of runny noses and chilly recesses, people can become lost. Sometimes; in the rush for touchdowns and Readin', Ritin', and 'Rithmetic; generations can be lost. We have to be careful with our children; they don't have the time or patience to throw their coats over their heads. Love of learning is too easy to extinguish even when the goals sought are relevant to the needs of an individual, and, more so, when what is being taught is clearly a waste of time.

At mid-year, we moved to Greeley and put Kristin back into the Community Center where they were observant enough to notice that she already knew how to put on her coat. She spent the rest of the school year there and was so successful they recommended she be transferred to the public school district where she could be in an educable special education class.

She spent the next five years in Greeley public schools where, among other fantastic feats, while mainstreamed for a part of her day into a first-grade class she had the starring role in a play entitled "The Crying Princess" (she got to be the princess), and she fell in love with a handsome young man named Mark. She learned how to count, to add, to subtract, to read. She learned to love going to school. Those were days filled with good teachers, good programs, mean kids on the playground who would pull off her wig, and a cluster of good friends about her— children gathered from all over the school district and assembled in a classroom where the teaching was paced at the right speed, and where they could shelter each other in friendship and understanding of the special nature of their existences.

The days would often start at home with my guitar and questionable voice singing a song that I wrote for her.

Kristin's Getting Dressed

Kristin's getting dressed,
she wants to look her best,
'cause it's a school day,
school day.
She's tying up her shoes,
she going to smile away her blues,
'cause it's a school day,
school day.

When she gobbles down her food,
it's not that she is rude,
it's just a school day,
school day.
She wipes the Krispies from her chin,
and gives the world another grin,
'cause it's a school day,
school day.

It's worth the hurry and the fuss,
when she's running for her bus,
'cause it's a school day,
school day.

From when it starts until it ends,
she spends the whole day with her friends,
'cause it's school day,
school day.

   I would stand next to her bed and get louder as I sang the verses, and she would pretend to be asleep the first time through and then jump up and sing along with me for the second time. She honestly loved getting up and getting ready for school. It's a special and delicate state of mind when a child enjoys learning and continues to do so for years.
   But, there was a short time in Greeley when she temporarily lost her enthusiasm. She was bright and was

excited about learning and, thus, a perfect subject for an experiment by the school district's special education department. It was decided that selected children with a variety of handicapping conditions could benefit from attending their neighborhood schools, rather than being bussed to schools that were sometimes miles away from their homes. The idea was to have resource centers located in schools that would service the special needs of all the students in the attendance area who were disabled physically, emotionally, or intellectually. The principle behind the change might have been financially motivated, but, nevertheless, Carol and I agreed to allow them to use Kristin as one of their guinea pigs. We were proud that they had chosen her.

The experiment failed terribly. The reason for its failure is important.

Kristin started the new school year with optimism and excitement. She thought it was neat that she was going to a school that was just a couple of blocks from home. She had looked forward to the experience and I thought it sounded pretty good myself. I was working at an appliance store as a Maytag man at the time and was able to walk to school with her before going to work. The walks were nice. We followed the side of a large field at the edge of our trailer court and then there was a sidewalk that ran along the road to the school. It was autumn-cool mornings and songs and silliness all the way. I would leave her off at the front door of the school and then sing and silly myself back home and go to my job with a good feeling about our mornings.

Carol would pick her up in the afternoon and when she would ask her about school Kristin always told her it was going fine. When I would get home from work and would say, "How was school, Kid?" she would say, "Great, Dad." Parents love to hear that things are going well for their children. Sometimes we like to hear it so much that we don't get around to finding out whether it is true. Kristin knew she was making us happy when she told us school was still wonderful. Our happiness has always been important to Kristin. In this case it was so important that she was reluctant to tell us just how miserable her days were at the new school. We noticed that she had started chewing her fingernails.

We received a note from one of her teachers saying that Kristin had been having behavior problems in the lunchroom. We scheduled a conference and went to talk to her. "Problems" it turned out, consisted of such things as throwing food and spitting water on other children. This was bizarre behavior for our kid who loved school. It took us a while to figure out what was wrong.

She had good teachers. It was a beautiful building full of bright colors and wooden work tables and learning centers. There was a staff that was friendly and kind to her. The external situation looked good, but it was missing a vital element. With all the good intentions and knowledge available to modern man, they had overlooked an ingredient which is critical to emotional stability: Kristin had no peer group.

Kristin spent her days without a friend. There was plenty to learn and good people to teach her. There were some kids who were nice to her and let her try to play their fast running games. But there was no one in that entire school with whom she could really talk, or giggle, or freely communicate. There is something special about Kristin and her friends. Something that even I, with all my years of hovering about the edge of her existence, can't begin to know. Among the clustered children, gathered from the far reaches of society and bonded together in a union of common need, there is an articulate mutuality of expression that fills her days with the metaphor of diverse human beings touching each other.

All living people seek to be complete. Each of us, regardless of limitation or distraction from the mainstream of our species, has a complex of needs that must be accounted for if frustration is to be kept at bay. Elements of the human heart/mind/spirit have got to be accommodated if any individual is to have a chance at a reasonably happy existence. Any social, educational, or personal situation that doesn't allow for such needs will fail. There was nowhere in the system of her day for Kristin to openly and comfortably communicate with fellow human beings who spoke her language, laughed at her jokes, and felt a common sense of isolation from a society that was only compassionate and could not possibly be empathetic.

"How was your day today, Kid?"

"Great, Dad."

"Who'd you talk to?"

"Teachers."

"Any kids?"

"Sure. Kind of."

"Want to go back to your old school with Mrs. Anderson and Steven and Mark and Lori and your other friends?"

"YES!"

I was at the Air Force Academy in Colorado Springs this past May. Kristin was participating in state Special Olympics gymnastics competition. I was standing on one side of the gym waiting for her turn to do her floor routine. Carol was on the other side of the large mat. We both had cameras and wanted to photograph as much of her performance as possible.

Over the past several years we have attended numerous Special Olympic events and maybe this is a good time to talk about some of the experiences I've had, some of the scenes I've witnessed, some of the perspective that I've gained by going to them. It ties into education eventually so I'm not straying too far from the topic of this chapter.

Kristin, primarily under the wondrous energies of Pat Miller of the South Suburban Recreations District, has run, jumped, swam, bowled, skated, and tumbled her way across years of special competition that have gained her ribbons and medals and a sense of winning and the thrill of trying. When she was a tiny little kid, she was entered into a track event in Greeley. I can still see her standing on the starting line with a big grin on her face as she waited for the race to begin. The starter said, "On your marks, get set," and then BANG! He shot the starting pistol and

43

Kirstin sat down and cried. The first time at anything is not easy. They started the race over for her and the nice man put his pistol aside and rather quietly said, "Go," to commence the twenty-five-yard dash down the chalked lanes to a fantastic second place and a red ribbon that she still has on a shelf in her room.

Kristin and I are not the die-hard competitors that much of our society encourages, and, while we are likely to reel in the "joy of victory," we seldom feel a real sense of "agony" in defeat, particularly when the game is as insignificant as running a race or bowling a strike. However, we do try our best. She and I consider sports as a potential source of a good time—not a test of our worthiness as human beings. But, when she's winning, or coming in second, or thrashing her heart out trying to keep up with the lithe figures of long-armed competitors ahead of her in the pool, I become as crazed as any "little league mother" in America.

In Special Olympics, disabled people are protected from the stampede of normal people who win so many of the races in the real world where it's open season on finishing lines. Within the stadiums on the days set aside for Kristin's people there are different rules, different standards. I heard a crowd roar at seeing a twenty-year old man do a standing broad jump of six inches. And it was not a patronizing cheer; it was as sincere as any shout the stadium had ever heard. On these special days, not only are there different standards for the participants, but there are also adjustments automatically made by those who observe. The reason this works is that, though world records for performance are seldom challenged at such events, there is no modification needed to allow for a diminished capacity regarding the presence of the human spirit.

I was waiting for them to call Kristin's name. She had been practicing for months on her own, down in her basement apartment where she mixes break dancing and cartwheels and has developed both coordination and physical poise. I was nervous because it was a giant gymnasium, and there were judges with official score boards and, for her sake, I wanted her to do well. She wasn't nervous at all. She knows that she is great.

I was standing next to some chairs where participants were awaiting their moment in the arena. I was listening to a couple of young people who were obviously much in love. The young man was nervous and chattered on to his girlfriend. She was trying to assure him that he would do fine. It meant so much to him to do well and she held his hand. They were probably in their early twenties and were in love. They giggled easily because he was nervous and she was nervous for him.

His time came and I watched as he walked to the parallel bars where he was to perform. He was heavy and his gait was uneven. He looked very serious. I watched as he falteringly supported himself and with rocking motions flopped his legs over the bars in a pattern that unsteadily progressed him to the far end of the bars where he unevenly settled himself to the floor and raised his arms in stumbling completion. There was applause and he headed back toward his chair. His lady friend was waiting for him. She was standing and there were tears in her eyes as she hugged him and said, "Oh, Ronnie, you looked so good." And he blushed.

I'll tell you what all this has to do with education. When situations arise for which standard philosophies are insufficient, we have to find alternate means of explaining the phenomena that confront us. There are many times when despair can be allayed only by systems of thought prefaced with "perhaps" and punctuated with a need to believe. Somewhere out there in the infinite range of "perhapses" there might even be some right answers.

Perhaps it is that each of us with our senses is a window of the collective consciousness of our species, or our universe. What each of us sees, hears, feels is part of the absolute of the universe. My perception is a trillionth of "all" but a finite necessary in the completion of the infinite. Perhaps the young lady's love-touched vision of her Ronnie superbly mounting the parallel bars and flawlessly executing his routine is a necessary part of that which becomes everything.

That's why the world must be as big as possible for everyone.

There is a man who works for Kristin's school district who is in charge of vocational education for special education students. I've talked to him on several occasions and he is a well-meaning, sincere individual who would like to provide the best training for the students he represents. When school started in the fall, when Kristin was fourteen, he proposed that she become involved in a vocational program that would take her out of school for several hours each week. He had lined up an opportunity for her to push a broom and clean toilets at a local community college. It would require that she miss some of her time in academic subjects, but he thought the work experience would be more valuable for her.

Let's take a poll. How many of you parents, regardless of the intellectual abilities of your children, like the idea of Jimmy, Jr. or little Amy or whatever you call the product of your loins being nose-level to a goddamned urinal with a scrub brush? Let's see those hands, raise them high so I can count them all. It's reality. Someone has got to clean the toilets of America if we are to maintain a decent level of civilization. I've done it and I've spent long hours looking down the shaft of a broom handle at the long aisles of warehouses. I've done it and taken pride in the shining product of my labors. There is no indignity to the profession. It's just not what most moms and dads dream of for their children. Few children fulfill the visions of their parents but, without some vision, what would any of us be? Kristin might end up with a job pushing a broom and I'll be proud of her for doing it. But, life's drudgery need not begin at fourteen. Life's chore of dealing directly with the task of earning a living will demand enough of her existence. I can see no advantage in starting the process prematurely, especially at the expense of learning about her world in social studies, learning to express herself better in English, learning to marvel at the wonders of the human body in science, and learning how to manipulate numbers in math.

Schools are full of the non-essential wonders of the world that have little to do with vocational determination. I've been an English teacher, a truck driver, a Maytag man, a poet: never in the application of my mind and body to making a living have I had need for a knowledge of how many bones are in my body or an understanding of the concept of invisible lines of latitude and longitude dividing up the sphere upon which I exist. I don't need to know the names of continents, or cloud formations, but I have the right to know about them because they make me more aware of my world. They have given me a more extensive perspective of my existence. It was my right to learn the marvelous scope of the non-essential so that I might better assess the essential. It was my right and it is the right of my child as well.

Perhaps the Universe needs Kristin's perception as a part of completing itself. It's important that she learn all she can before she heads out to a world of brooms and time clocks and other essentialities.

Kristin, like all of us who desire a full life, must find the world to be a continually expanding entity of her perception. There will always be plenty left to learn.

Last fall she and I were driving out of the parking lot of our favorite Mexican restaurant. We had enjoyed a fine meal of Taco House's famous forty-cent enchiladas and were feeling good when, with the white-grey sky enveloping the early autumn dusk, she said, "Serious clouds."

"What did you say?' I asked.

"Seri . . . serio . . . ser—I don't know.

"Cirrus?"

"Yeah, cirrus clouds," she said with exuberance.

And I laughed like a wild man and there were tears in my eyes and I hugged her as we swerved up the street.

"Those are cirrus clouds," she repeated.

"Yes," I said, "serious clouds."

She's fifteen and she's pretty, and at her school they have finally come to realize that it is her right to know some of the nonessential wonders of the world—about the equator and about the sky and about the seas. Now she can name the continents, though she has an awful time trying to say Antarctica. She knows about ears and lungs and about the history of her town. She loves to tell about the gold seekers and the farmers. She loves to know things and to tell them.

She's come a hell of a long way for a *vegetable,* a *nonhuman.*

Kristin's World

It's never easy to project yourself into someone else's world, no matter how close you feel that you are to his or her reality. But, I'm going to try.

Her world is important to us all because the quality of her life can be an index to the status of the health of our culture. The way that we deal with her difficulties and the difficulties of her peers can be indicative of the state of compassion within the flux of our asserted image in the world. In other words, Kristin's world—as facilitated by our government, our schools, our cultural mores, our values as a nation of diverse consumers of a single and vastly accessible K-Mart Blue Light Special—is a measure of America's true identity. I've already mentioned that mean kids would pull off her wig out on the playground. I'm still pissed off about that happening to my kid, and, even though she has explained to me many times that it was better for her to live with such treatment than to get into trouble for kicking the little brats in the *cajones*, I'm not sure that I agree. The fact that "mean kid" has such generic implications in Kristin's world angers and disturbs me.

This is why I'll have to rely upon Kristin's help in this section. She's no Pollyanna, but she's usually not as enraged about her world as I am. I think that she likes her world and that makes me happy. We'll tell you about it: People, school, music, tomorrow.

I'll tell you about one of the eight thousand ways in which I perceive Kristin's world.

For four years I taught in an alternative education program within a public junior high school. The program was designed to meet the needs of a normally distributed group of seventh grade students. By using interdisciplinary

49

teaching techniques, community resources, group assessment of individual needs, field trips, and a hell of a lot of our own time and emotional resources, we four teachers were attempting to lessen the trauma of our students in adjusting to junior high school and adolescence, while providing a thorough academic program that approximated the curriculum used by the rest of the seventh-grade teachers. And, contrary to the inferences of some, we were not a bunch of ungodly, flesh-worshipping secular humanists. We did share a common belief in the basic worthiness of the human complex and also a belief that, with proper nurturing and careful examination, elements of the finer qualities of the human species could be discovered in twelve- and thirteen-year-old-kids.

As part of this program, every fall, in late September or early October, we would take our students on a three- or four-day camping trip to a forested area about fifty miles from the school. On such outings it became possible for teachers and students to get to know one another and to share memorable experiences together. We conducted school out in the woods and tried to make the best use of nature in our approaches to math, English, social studies, and science. The math teacher talked about geometric shapes in nature and used proportion to measure the height of a tree by its shadow. The social studies teacher took the kids to a graveyard and talked about local history and epidemics and infant mortality. The science teacher did a lesson on geology while the kids climbed through crevices made by freezing and thawing and erosion and gravity. As the resident English teacher/poet, it was my responsibility to use nature as a means of dealing with creative expression.

The first year I did this, Kristin was ten years old. She was doing all right, but those weren't easy times for her. I was miles away in the woods with a group of kids who needed to learn about their own compassion and their own power. I saw it as an opportunity to affect some potential "mean kids" for their own behalf as well as Kristin's.

I took them on a three-mile hike and made stops along the way. During the walk no one was allowed to talk except me. We listened to the sounds of our feet crossing dirt roads and pine-needle forest floors, and our legs as they brushed through dry grass meadows and dew-damp shadowy glades. We smelled the pine trees and felt the Indian summer breezes. We heard birds and insects and in four years of taking those hikes with sixteen groups of twenty-five to thirty children, I had to tell only one kid to shut up.

At each stop I would talk about absorbing the sensory input, which was heightened by our silence. I talked about the need for creativity in everyone's life. And on the second stop I would tell them about Kristin.

I would start by telling them nothing about what they were going to hear except that it was a form of creative expression based upon an individual's need to present a personal message in a way that others could understand. It was a work of fiction, a creative expression, based upon real feelings and real needs. I would then tell them that Charles Darwin was a scientist who, among others, developed a theory that in nature only the strongest members of a species survive. Then I would read them the following short story:

Darwin

It was in the high country. Up the steep Rockies where spring is a green and luscious moment followed by a short summer and autumn, and then the snow. Some had told him it was no place to raise a family but he wanted his children to be strong—to learn to combat the powers of nature as well as he had. And, also, he considered the comfort and convenience of towns and cities to be corrupt.

So he built the cabin high up where the hunting and trapping were good and where the talkers and deceivers of the towns were far away

51

and nearly forgotten for most of the year. The cabin was built with great care from the huge trees that surrounded his mountain meadow. Each log was carefully and closely fitted into the next. The cabin was heavy and tight—snug against the blizzard-cold winds. It sat in a meadow at the base of giant trees near the pine-needle floor of the forest.

There was a stream that wrapped around the clearing and washed and sang through spring and summer and bubbled beneath the white hard ice in late fall and winter. It gave them fish to eat and clean cool water to drink.

It was there, amidst the eternal green of the forest and the whites of winter snows and the aspen shades of summer and fall, that he would raise his small family to be as he was—strong, resourceful, independent, and at peace with the ebb and flow of the seasons and the elements of nature. His children would learn the qualities which had made it possible for him to survive in the beautiful, yet hostile world of the distant mountains. And his pretty wife Amy believed his dream and was as resolute in living it as was he.

The first two babies were perfect. As he drew them with his rugged hands from the warmth of his wife, he felt their tight, resilient muscles and listened to the shrill strong sound of their first air-rushed cries. They would be good men, both of them, and he started them early on the path of strength he knew so well.

Amy still wanted a girl. Someone to whom she could pass on her own feminine strength and wisdom. Someone to rear in her own fine form of humor and sensitivity and endurance. Someone to whom she could teach her skills. And, also, she wanted the company of another female in the isolated world of the high country.

The pregnancy was normal and Amy had no trouble the whole time. She never felt the need to ease up on her work. If anything, she seemed to enjoy the everyday tasks that filled her days more than ever before. What had been monotonous had developed new meaning, new purpose. The demands of creating a home and caring for the children and her husband had taken on a certain quality which had been previously lacking. Amy sensed the little girl growing within her and eagerly awaited her arrival. Her songs were light and her movements graceful as she performed her half of the rituals of survival for the family.

Susan would be her name and she would form herself in the image of Amy, the same as the boys were shadowing the example of their father.

It was late spring and the meadow was covered with deep green grass down the bank of the stream. The boys were growing perfectly. They spent their days learning the ways of their father, and when they played they romped like puppies through the deep grass. Amy would watch from the cabin porch with sewing on her lap or from the kitchen window while preparing meals.

The familiar pressure began and Sam stayed home from his traps. The boys were kept quiet but they watched as their mother twisted and moaned upon the bed. Sam stood by her and would speak soft words to her and she would smile from far away and whisper to the boys not to worry.

Susan was born in the early hours of morning when light was a gray haze in the sky and vision was the perception of silhouettes. The boys were sleeping and Amy was exhausted after many hours of labor. Sam was worn with the long hours and the tension of his wife's pain.

From the first moment that Sam touched his daughter, he knew that something was wrong. Something was wrong in the limpness of her tiny arms, in the feel of her neck. The boys had been tense little balls of energy exploding with life; she was flaccid and still. He held her up and there was no cry. He struck her and only a slight murmur arose from her lips. He struck her again and again with his strong hand trying to break loose the great power that had lurked within the tiny lungs of his sons. But only the faintest sounds emerged.

Amy watched through the half light and knew by his actions and by the standards of their existence that she had failed. She stretched her tired arms towards Sam and took the frail baby from his desperate hands, and held her close.

It was another spring and then another. The seasons worked their time upon the mountain family. The boys were becoming strong and responsible in their simple years. They gathered wood and walked the forest with their father. They played games in the meadow grasses and along the swiftly running stream.

Amy and Susan stayed close to the cabin for it was only with the continuous protection of the home and with the attention of almost all of Amy's time that the weak child had survived the effect of two vicious winters. Amy's attentions and Sam's and the boy's vigilance at the fire had carried little Susan through the shallow-breath gasping of pneumonia and burning, weakening fevers.

They had expected the tiny girl to die within minutes of her birth, but somehow she had continued to breathe and then to take nourishment from the breasts of her mother.

They watched her constantly for the first days. Sam left his traps to the beasts and watched his daughter live.

Amy dedicated her whole being to the preservation of Susan's fragile existence. Sam continued the activities that maintained the needs of their lives, but there were many interruptions to the gathering of food and fuel to check on the condition of the baby. When the snows came that first year there was less food in the larder than ever before. There had not been so much time to hunt, to prepare the meat. The baby needed all of the attention any of the family could spare. That winter the boys were sick for the first time in their lives and Sam knew that the scarcity of their meals was the cause of their susceptibility.

Susan started coughing with the first chilling night and even as she played in tiny movements in her crib, they saw her weakening.

Twice that winter Sam rode through bitter cold nights and blowing snows to the distant town. And each time, the medicine that he brought back from the doctor did little to improve her condition.

Susan was sick the whole winter, but she lived. That spring she sat with Amy on the porch and watched the boys playing their games in the deep spring grass and down the rushing stream. She wanted to play but the grass was too damp, the air too cool.

The full frigid force of the second winter arrived and Susan was no stronger. Again, it took all of their efforts to keep the fires always roaring and the doors and windows always sealed against the slightest breeze. The doctor was consulted several more times that winter but all of his medicines were ineffective.

She lived again, but, when the snow had melted except in shadowed patches, and the sprigs of grass were breaking through the moist ground, she was weaker than she had been the previous spring.

It wasn't something that they talked about, yet it was something that they all knew, even the boys. No one really had to say it. It was obvious that tiny Susan with her blowing soft hair and her pale blue eyes and white face could never survive another winter. The family was being consumed in the preservation of the weak child, and for naught. She had not the strength to live.

Late spring had arrived and the grass was thick and wet following a morning rainstorm. By late afternoon the sky had cleared and was intensely blue. The boys were playing their hunting games by the stream as the slanting sunlight gave a brilliant glow to the fresh green grasses. Susan watched with her mother from the porch. With pleading eyes and motions she begged to join the laughing boys down the meadow by the stream. Amy held her back—the grass was so damp and the wind so cool.

Sam watched them from the corner of the porch.

The boys were in the grass then—crashing and crawling through its softness—drenching themselves as they rolled and wrestled through the rain-specked blades.

Susan pulled at her mother's enwrapping arms.

And then, with a glance at Sam and no words, Amy let her go.

I would let the silence sit for a moment or two as I folded my copy of the story and put it into the back pocket of my jeans. The quiet would allow those who understood the meaning of the story to absorb its impact, and those who didn't to question what they had missed. I would let them think for a long minute, and then I would speak.

"It's not an easy story. It's about the power of nature and its beauty and its impersonal cruelty. It's about the death of a weak child.

"Creativity allows us to combine things that are known by many people with things that only we know, and in doing so express difficult ideas or truths. We all know about the power of nature. It was cold last night in our campground and the wind spoke with howling might through the pine trees. We all know something of the chill of winter snows and the barking of the dark night beasts across our awarenesses.

"I'll tell you where stories come from. They come from a writer's need to express his or her thoughts to as many people as possible. Writers need to describe experiences that are common to their readers if they are to be able to successfully tell their stories.

"I needed to tell this story in such a manner that you could understand its message. I needed to talk about powers and situations that threatened the existence of a disabled child.

"I know about the fierce cold of winter. So do you.

"I know about the impersonal turns of the icy winds of nature that surround us all. So do you.

"And I know the fears and the needs of a small weak child in a huge and often cruel world. And I needed to tell people about that child and about the world that awaits her. I could have written about an abnormal child's life in a normal world, but what do any of us here know about the terror of the forces that swirl about us, when we are so capable of dealing with them?

"We all can run fast, can think quickly, can usually cope with the energies that form our world.

"I needed to create an environment that was threatening to everyone if I expected anyone to understand my story.

"Let me translate the symbols of this story for you. The little girl in this story is my daughter. She was born weak into a world of howling cold winds, death-chilling snows. And the winds, the snows, the circling death—you are the winds, the snows; we are the cold; all of us who sit in this forest meadow today and contemplate the forces of nature are the causes of the fear and death that surround my kid as she walks out the front door and climbs onto her school bus each morning.

"And we are not bad people, nor is the winter wind a malicious force. Most of us have seldom, if ever, intentionally tried to harm or frighten or terrorize a helpless person. But all of us have had our victims.

"My kid can't run as fast as any of you. She can't add or subtract or multiply as accurately as you. And the words of her books come slowly into the comprehension of her mind. She could be easy prey to the gathering wolves. But she's not.

"She's my child and she is strong of spirit and she is pretty and her being is as magnificent as that of any of you. Her place upon this planet is as important. And to us who can be so carelessly cruel with our words and mocking actions, she is forgiving.

"I read you this story because you need to know where stories come from and why they are important to tell if we are to communicate our individual truths. But, also, I read it to you in hopes that you will become more aware of the terrible might of our casual, everyday powers. I want my kid to have a nice life, and you can help make it possible."

* * * *

I believe in the basic goodness of the human spirit. But, I'm no damn fool either. I work in hallways where words like "fag" and "dick" and, of course, "retard" are common expressions of insecurity and confused rage. There are teachers in my building who use the expression "retard" in describing students who make foolish mistakes. I'll never tell Kristin that it is going to be easy. To say so would be a deception, even in the best of human environments.

It was late at night in mid-August several years ago. Kristin and I were sitting out on the fourteenth-floor balcony of Carol's apartment overlooking the lights and sparse traffic of Denver. We were out there drinking Kool-Aid and talking about life. She knows a lot about life.

I asked her what she thought about starting junior high school at the end of the month, and she told me she was excited about the idea of going to a new school. She has always liked the idea of getting older—of growing up. It has always worried me. I knew the way junior high school kids talked and thought and how mean they could be in just joking around with each other, and how with beast-like patterns, they can insidiously encircle the weak. Carol and I both had felt anxious about Kristin's being subjected to such an infamous environment. "It's going to be great, Dad. I'll have more friends and I'll learn lots of stuff."

"Has anyone ever called you names at school?" I asked.

Kristin became very serious. There are always issues surrounding us that we acknowledge but seldom discuss. She took a long sip of Kool-Aid and said, "Sure. The mean kids called me names."

"What did they call you?"

"Bad words."

"Like what?"

"Bitch."

"And . . . "

"Retard."

"What do you feel like when they call you those names?"

"It makes me mad."

"Do you cry?"

"Sometimes."

"Do you ever kick them in the balls when they call you names?"

"Dad... "

"I mean it. Have you ever pulled their perfect little hair after they pulled your wig off?"

"No."

59

"Why not?"

"I'm not a bad person."

"What do you do when they make fun of you and hurt your feelings?"

"I tell them that it's not nice to call people names. I tell them to leave me alone."

"Do they?"

"Sometimes. Sometimes the teachers tell them to leave me alone."

"It makes me mad, too, Kristin. Real mad."

"Yeah."

There are billions of worlds on this planet. Behind each living face there is a separate world full of energy and needs and perceptions. In each world there is all of the importance of experience and personal priority and emotion that exists. When a small child cries from a heart full of sorrow, it is, in that moment, all the sorrow in the world.

"I hope that junior high school is all right for you."

"Don't worry, Dad. It's going to be neat."

Time has passed. This year she is in her third and final year at Euclid Junior High School. It's her world and when she says it's going to be great, it is great. Years of learning and laughing and lunchtime trauma. Giggling loves and gaping losses. Friends and fantasies, rock and roll. Adolescent truth: It's hers and she takes it all in.

I'll tell you what I know about her life, again, so that we can judge the health of our society.

Kristin is a bowler, swimmer, ice skater, tennis player, gymnast, break-dancer. She can throw darts and sings songs either spontaneously created, memorized, or approximated along with the radio. Honest tears have been known to well up in the eyes of listeners as she and I have crooned "Tennessee Waltz" in two-part harmony (though I'm not certain of what emotions were at play in producing them). Her expressions about culture are a collage of heroes and favorites. She loves good movies but hates too much violence. Her favorite actors are Harrison Ford and George Burns. Michael Jackson, Bob Segar, and, lately, Bruce Springsteen are the current musical wonders of her life. A profile of her cultural preferences would likely be quite similar to those of many fifteen-year-old young ladies in America.

She and Carol went to the Michael Jackson concert in 1984. Tens of thousands of screaming, cheering, crying fans and Kristin right there in the middle of them in the full swoon of the electric night.

She likes her clothes to be bright and pretty. She likes the privacy of her own room and respect for her tastes in entertainment. When she listens to rock and roll or watches MTV videos, the house could be on fire and she wouldn't notice.

Sound like a lot of kids you know?

She's just like a million kids and not like any of them.

We were eating marvelous cheeseburgers at Bud's Tavern in Sedalia one afternoon after I had picked her up at the bowling alley. We had been laughing and singing all the way down the fourteen-mile road from Littleton. It was an exceptional spring afternoon packed with hope and warm air and a gentle sun. Kristin and I were talking about writing. She had written a fairy tale the year before and wanted to start another book.

Her first work was called *Queen Kristin*. It's about a witch name Grouch who, with the magical incantation, "Icky, wicky, sticky, do—I'm gonna put a spell on you," made all the trees in Tree Country vanish. It was a great little book. I've got a copy of it, bound in green paper with thread-sewn binding in the lid compartment of my brief case. Carol and she gave it to me as a Father's Day gift. They had worked for over a month with Kristin telling her ideas and Carol typing them. Whenever I'm digging through my briefcase looking for vital documents, or grade books, or a clean pair of socks and I see its shiny green cover, I feel proud.

"Do you want to write another work of fiction or do you want to try nonfiction this time?" I asked. "Do you want to make up a story like you did in your first book or do you want to tell a true story?"

She thought a moment and then said, "I think a true story."

"Good," I said. "What do you want to write about?"

Again she pondered for a bit before she spoke. "I don't know. Maybe I'll write about my friends."

She thought for a moment and said, "I think a true story."

"That's a good idea. You've got some nice friends. What do you want to say about them?"

"I want to write about how nice they are and how fun it is to know them. I want to tell how funny Jimmy is and about how I tease Ben and call him Benjamin. And I want to write about Annie and me."

"And . . ."

"Yeah, I'll write about Tom and how cute he is," and she giggled.

"What else do you want to say?"

"I want to write about the other kids in my class, too. Like Sam who sometimes I push around in a wheelchair and Bret who lies down all day. I want to write about my friends who need help."

And I thought about her friends and how someone needs to tell their stories and said, "That's a wonderful idea. What do you want to call your new book?"

Without any hesitation she said, *People Who Need Help.*

We were so excited about the idea that we ordered another Budweiser and a Seven-Up with two cherries so each of us could have one. *People Who Need Help,* I repeated. "It's a great idea, Kristin."

"I want people to understand."

"Understand what?"

"There are people who need help and other people need to understand about them."

"Kristin!" I said with elation. "You've just written the first line of your book."

We finished our hamburgers and then we ate the whole side dish full of pickles and onions that came with the meal. It was such an evening.

"Are you going to write about yourself, Kristin?" I asked.

"What do you mean?"

It wasn't an easy question to ask but I did. "Aren't you one of the people who need help?"

"Sometimes."

"And Tom, and Annie, and Ben . . .?"

"Sometimes."

She looked at me and gathered her thoughts and said, "I still don't know what you mean."

"I mean, don't you need a little more help than some of the other kids at your school? Like with your math and reading?"

"Yeah."

"That's what I mean." There is so much that is not spoken.

Then her eyes formed another question. A question that, yet, repeatedly speaks through my mind with Kodachrome clarity.

"Dad," she said, "am I a handicapped?"

How much do you tell a kid about her limitations without overly reinforcing them? What level of reality can any of us stand when it directly affects every action of our lives? Some of the psychological trends of the last few years have emphasized dealing with the real world, but I think many of us wage a better battle for our own mental health using some of the escape mechanisms that have protected us through the years—sheltering our egos in a sea of ego killers.

She asked, "Am I a handicapped?" There are people who accurately maintain that all of us are handicapped in one way or another, and it is only a matter of the degree or pertinence of our handicaps that determines our status in a not so "normal" world. I could have told her that all of us

63

are handicapped. But I think, in the context of our conversation, I would have been lying to her, or at least rationalizing to her. My good friend, Carol Ann More, a fine spokesperson for physically and mentally limited individuals, raises hell with me for using the term "handicapped" at all. She vehemently insists from the podium of her electric wheelchair that the proper term is "disabled," and the etymology of "handicapped" leads back to the demeaning pose of people using their "caps" to beg for sustenance. She is a proud and beautiful lady and she is right. I could have told Kristin that "handicapped" is not the right word, but at the moment down at Bud's Tavern I don't think semantics was the most important subject we were discussing.

We were talking about Kristin's perception of herself.

"Are you handicapped?" I repeated her question.

"Yeah, Dad."

Such a question to answer. Such words.

"Yes, Kristin. You are handicapped."

I don't think she was unaware of the fact that she was different from the mainstream of her culture, but I'm not sure she had ever directly confronted her "label" in this culture in which she lives.

Smart kid.

You see, she and I have talked about being different for years. Predating the earliest harassments of her life, I had started telling her it was all right to be different and that people who had trouble accepting different people were weak and were to be pitied (and sometimes kicked in the balls). I have told her all of these years that she and I were alike in that we don't easily fit into the roles and molds of the storybook bullshit that is the myth of our world. "We are not like other people, Kristin," I would tell her. "You and I won't ever be like other people and that's the way it is. We aren't necessarily better, but we certainly are different. Different in our minds, different in our hearts. And we're as good as any other people on the planet."

I've never fit into any corner of society in my life. Kristin fits only into a small and misunderstood niche of "people who need help." "I am a poet," I would tell her. "And you are the daughter of a poet. We are not like other people. We are different."

I guess I never had taken the step of telling her that a part of her difference was due to her being mentally disabled. I knew it, Carol knew it, and I'm certain that Kristin knew it. It hadn't seemed that important within the context of our lives together. She was a unique entity because she was the child of unique parents, not because of a screwed-up set of chromosomes.

'Yes," I had told her. She was handicapped.

I seem to have lost track of my main idea in developing this section—to tell you about Kristin's world. There's a good reason for this. It's her perception; it's her story to tell. All I can report are the symptoms of her existence. The outward appearances that are available to my awareness. The inward feelings that I sense as a loving father, as a poet, as a human receptor for the messages of my species. To get the real scoop you'll have to read her book, *People Who Need Help,* that is, true to the procrastinating nature of the child of a poet, still hovering on the verge of creation just a couple of taps of the space bar beyond its first line. I'm sure that she will eventually write it, just as I am sure that I will eventually complete this work myself. (Soon I hope—we could all use the royalties and I think the world could use the words.)

I'll tell you about the symptoms of Kristin's life. She laughs a lot. Good, hearty, frivolous, life-deep laughter. When she is giddy, the world should be giddy. When she laughs at her dog, a strange little cacophony of breeding, it is because he is being a funny little beast. There is no lack in discernment in her perception of humor. (Though sometimes there is a definite lack of discretion as demonstrated by the riotous laughter which often follows the mild mishaps of my life such as bashing my head into overhanging lamps or stumbling over telephone cords.) She has a good laugh—full of survival.

She seems to accept life on the terms given her from birth. At times she is angry, hurt, or excessively pensive;

but I don't believe she gets exceptionally depressed. She sees the world as a nice place with a few rough edges, not as the jagged son of a bitch that I sometimes see for her. Her view of life is an honest appraisal based upon having loving parents, concerned and affectionate teachers and other adults in her life, and upon the fact that she has almost always had good friends to stave off the vast and lonely potential of each impersonal day.

She's not the stereotypical grinning child who, by the self-deception of normal observation has been traditionally described as "always happy." Mentally disabled people are generally not "always happy." Kristin is a person of moods and irrationalities as much as any of us. She's lucky in that whatever has constituted the elements of her growth has not left her unduly contemplative of what is wrong with existence. She usually is able to speak a sincere good word for the plain of being we all share as well as for that singular level which is her own.

People who are around Kristin long enough to accept her wisdom often find themselves looking at their own worlds with a somewhat more positive posture. She's hauled my old caboose out of the swamps of my own despair on many occasions.

There are days when she is crabby, obstinate, bitchy, weird, irate, or any combination of the above. There are days when I stay the hell away from her because she pisses me off. There are days when she takes particular pleasure in driving me nuts. I'll not waste your time describing an idealized version of a real human being. Kristin is real and, believe me, she inflicts the full range of human communication upon her environment. She's a country mile from perfect, but, from as impartial a view as a dad can have of his daughter, I think she's the best.

Kristin's world is unjust, cruel, beautiful, ignorant, and enlightened. It is a world I occasionally attack as I have in this work, but which attacks her every day of her life. It is a world of songs and images full of the rhythms and colors exemplifying the fine spirit of the human race. In her world there is kindness and there is vicious harassment.

When short-sighted politicians selfishly manipulate the resources of an economy to the neglect of hunger and need, they squander the true wealth of that nation and undermine the heart of its people. My daughter does all right, but I don't believe the world is good enough for her yet. For Kristin and the millions of others who need help, we, as a culture, need to give freely of the funds of our hearts, our minds, and our material wealth. It can only enrich the lives and worth of us all.

The Future

Initially I thought that bringing up the bitterness and rage and sorrow of the past would be the most difficult part of this book. I was wrong.

The past I call a success, for it has led to the present; the present is justified by the vast symphony of intent, coincidence, intersection, and fortune which is the wake of even this very moment; the future is the amorphous realm of the shadows of my own self-doubt.

Yesterday has been suffered, relished, and absorbed. Today is a place of poetic sensitivity and richness that incorporates decades of perception. Tomorrow, in my most negative vision, is a place of non-existence, fraught with the prospect of illusions shattered.

Tomorrow could well be the best day of my life, of Kristin's life, of the world's life. I don't dread its dubious promise—for my own sake I see it as an adventure. But for Kristin, I know that it will be a time of reality supplanting the possibility of the realization of certain of the mundane dreams of normalcy. She'll not drive a car nor independently enjoy the accessibility of roads leading to undefined vistas; she'll not master the perplexing complexity of the Information Age. She will not bear a child. The cruelty of the future is brought about by the fact that she coexists with normalcy and shares its expectations. There are difficult truths that lie ahead for her. I'm her daddy and daddies don't like their little girls to be disappointed.

Basically, in her regard I am a coward...

Four years ago Kristin and Carol and I took a trip together out to the coast of Oregon. It was a wonderful time. We rented a place right on the ocean that had a kitchen and a huge front window. We walked for miles along the beach and over the sea-battered rocks. We all were happy and touched by the damp exhilaration of the ocean air and the good feelings of being together in a place so special as to be dreamlike at times—evening fog, golden spray of sunset surf, breathing voice of the earth.

And then one morning I found Kristin sitting on a driftwood log by herself. She was crying. I sat down next to her and put an arm around her and tried to comfort the sorrow that sobbed from her shaking body. I asked what was wrong and she couldn't tell me. Carol said that we should take a walk and we headed up the beach toward a distant point of black-rocked cliffs. Kristin kept at a distance and finally told us to go on without her. She said that she wanted to play in the sand.

We left her there. She had a stick and was making marks in the wet sand down where the outgoing waves had been. We continued on up the beach for about five minutes and then headed back toward her. We could see her small form in the distance—bent over, working industriously on the marks she was making in the sand. I said, "What the hell's wrong with Kristin, she's really acting weird."

And Carol had no answer.

When we got back to Kristin, she looked very serious and she pointed to a message she had written in large careful letters upon the beach.
It read:

> Dear Mom and Dad,
> Your kid is sad.
> Love,
>   Kristin

Late that afternoon I sat at the window looking out at the sea and Carol came out of the bathroom and said,

"Kristin has started menstruating." And without a moment's hesitation, without any cognitive or communicative process consciously in effect, I replied in a voice approaching outrage. "No! She has not!"

I'm a coward when it comes to my kid's future, and I'll bet I'm not the only one on this planet who has experienced such trepidation regarding his or her offspring. Any cynic who loves his kids is bound to be a little bit of a chicken for their sakes. Kristin isn't. She looks at her future the same way I look at mine. "It's going to be great," she tells me. For her, tomorrow is not a place where dreams die: It is a place where hopes and beliefs are actualized. Hell, she's been looking for her own apartment since she was nine-years old. It was then that she started breaking the sad news to me that she intended to have a place of her own... "but don't worry, Dad, you and Mom can visit me anytime you want—just call first."

I guess I never have really seen her future as a dismal prospect—just dangerous. She tells me that it's my problem and she's probably right.

I suppose my apprehension about Kristin's future can be construed as another example of "syndroming" her. It does seem somewhat contradictory for me to have written all of these pages pleading for fairness in her life, just to negate the whole process by dreading what could well be the best part of it.

I guess most parents feel as if time runs out before the job of rearing is completed. She's fifteen and, for the most part, her values, her sensitivities, her own set of apprehensions are probably set by now. She'll have three or four more years of school, including some form of vocational training that hopefully, will be consistent with her personal needs and special abilities; and then, it will be off to a life of work and people and the diverse experiences which will fill her distances.

Somewhere in close proximity to her existence, Carol and I, in our connected separateness with her, will be living our lives, doing our work, knowing our people, and maintaining a constant source of love and support for her

70

as long as we live. She will not be our burden, for she has never been such in our lives. She will continue to be a portion of the purpose of our beings—a significant portion for both of us.

Dilemmas and limitations are a part of every life. Either we face them or they run us under.

Kristin likely has as good a shot at happiness as any of us. It's always so personal anyway.

So, instead of trying to play soothsayer, I'll just stop here and hope, as all loving parents hope, that my daughter's life will be rich and rewarding.

And to those of you who encounter her, and those of you who outlive the help that we can provide for her, may you have the reward and joy of sharing a portion of her path, as we have. Be kind to Kristin and to all of the inhabitants of her special nation of "people who need help," for it is by the quality we provide their lives that we might measure the worth of our own hearts.

Update: March, 1987

It took a decade to write this book. I am self-publishing this work because it needs to be read. (And Kristin needs the work—I have hired her as my mail order department.)

I said that Kristin would never drive. Wrong.

Last June, on her sixteenth birthday, Carol and I took her up near the Wyoming border where roads are forever and traffic is sparse. There, witnessed by the wonder of coyotes, antelope, and fence-post crows, my young lady cruised over twenty miles of grassland farm lanes with hardly a hitch. Though one left turn proved to be somewhat more exciting than we intended, overall, Kristin did a fine job on her first day out upon the highways. If I'm ever rendered incapable of operating a vehicle by wild beasts, bad moonshine, or the culminating violence of decades of egg-abuse, I think she could do a decent job of driving me to help.

Some people have told me that I shouldn't have included the part about the "holy" teacher and my rage against Supreme Beings. They've told me that I might have offended readers when I describe God as "heartless." I regret if I alienate good people with my frankness, but I believe I would be doing a disservice to the honesty of this work by omitting such an important facet of my reactive rage.

Regarding the organization of this work (or seeming lack thereof), life is a collage of images and experiences, people and phenomena—an approximation at best. It was my intention to tell the poem of Kristin's times—not the chronology. There are subtleties of mood and shades of remembrance that assert themselves into all of our experiences. Seldom are we afforded the clarity of a truly isolated moment.

Kristin has a job. The same folks who projected vistas of gleaming white toilet sets a few years ago have coordinated a fine working experience for her now. Kristin works in a video store. For two hours on Mondays and Wednesdays, she sorts and restocks taped movies, collates brochures, and generally helps out behind the scenes. She loves it. Last Monday she received her first paycheck and it was a time of celebration. I wrote that the vocational education man was a good person—now I think he is a good person who has accomplished a good thing. I am thrilled by the idea of my daughter catching a city bus to go to a job where she is treated well and is learning to be useful while earning some money. I'm hoping that she'll buy breakfast for us on Saturday morning.

This July Kristin will participate in the International Special Olympics at Norte Dame University. A pretty young lady named Brenda and her assistant Pam have been working with her on gymnastics for over a year. Brenda translates a sport into an art, and mere movement into dance. Spinning in Kristin's cartwheels there is an essence of physical poetry that is a joy to observe. I've helped, too. I have told Kristin of the difference between a jump and a flight, the difference between performing and being. When I leap across the girth of her mat, I cease to be a two-hundred pound, stubby-legged, misplaced mountain man. I become music and light and poetry. Even if to an observer I have the grace of a middle-aged potato, I am beautiful. Kristin laughs when I end up a rubble of pulled parts and pain, heaped against the basement wall. But, when Kristin takes flight it is with well-practiced grace, and she carries with her the aerial spirit that is the momentary belief of all who rue the tyranny of gravity.

When Carol and Kristin are together and I hear their laughter and I sense the good harmony of their times, I know something of the cosmic songs which spin through the black-cold distances of the universe and give gifts to the emptiness. When the two of them risk the terror of scary movies on television, and I see Kristin peeking around the door jamb from the kitchen with eyes squinting nearly shut, and Carol on the living room couch tentatively peering over the hem of a blanket with fingers in her ears, I know that they are as one, these sweet ladies of my life. They've bought themselves a fine house with a full basement that, in another year or so, we will convert into an apartment for Kristin. She craves independence and the basement will be a good compromise arrangement for her. Carol has remained throughout these years and experiences as a companion to my soul. She and Kristin are the best friends I have.

On this twenty-fifth day of March 1987, I consider the precious elements of my life, and I envy no human being on the face of the earth.

The Kristin Book: Update 2013

To live...a life that shall love itself.

(Kristin Nichols / May 6, 1999)

It's been about twenty-six years since I published *The Kristin Book.* Wow. I must really be getting old. When her amazing story began, I was a twenty-five-year-old lad with all my hair, all my dreams, and no idea in the world what fatherhood was going to mean to me. Carol and I were overwhelmed by the devastating news of Kristin's unfortunate extra chromosome. I mean, we were mentally prepared for an eighteen- to twenty-one year run of responsibility and adulthood like we had inflicted upon our loving parents. After that stint of diapers, kindergarten plays, parent-teacher conferences, sports, boyfriends, emotional/social traumas, and celebrations, our baby was to have become a budding rocket scientist or published poet or rodeo clown or what have you, and that would do it.

When you are in your twenties, no matter how smart, educated, well-traveled, or street savvy you are, you really don't know diddlysquat. Life is the only true teacher, and life takes time.

On the morning of June 7, 1970, our lives were changed forever. This book has documented the first sixteen years of our experience with Kristin. Initially, she was our beautiful little child who seemed to have been born with a curse. I've told the story of her blossoming into the joy of our lives. Time has taught us that what Kristin brings to this world is hardly a curse; it is a blessing.

You know about her childhood and school and adolescence, wait until you hear about Kristin's life clear up into her forties. Hold on to your hats.

And that business about parenting being a limited obligation . . . nonsense. Until he passed a year or so ago, well into his ninety-seventh year, my old dad was still there for his kids.

"Say, Dad, I was wondering..."

"How much, Robert?"

For this brief update, I'm going to have Carol and Kristin contribute some of their words. For the three of us, it's been an amazing journey of miles and trials and mostly smiles. Join us. This is going to be fun.

When I wrote *The Kristin Book,* I tried to describe the experience from the viewpoint of each of us. Carol adds a deeper awareness of those, and ensuing times, in our lives from her perspective.

Carol's Thoughts

by

Carol Nichols

I'm not sure where to start when writing about Kristin and her life since the first edition of *The Kristin Book*. So, I'll just write some thoughts about what has developed over the decades since that first book. Now, over forty years since her birth, I still cringe when I think about our decision to leave her in the hospital to be turned over to a foster home. Hindsight is always clearer, but now it's absolutely impossible to imagine that we could have made that decision. There was extreme guilt when it happened and that morphed into a severe depression that lasted much longer. Over forty years later I still get upset thinking about it and I think of it often. While leaving her in the hospital after her birth was the worst decision we ever made, going to get her from the foster home and bringing her home with us was the best. As soon as she was old enough, we told Kristin about all this. She has never resented our awful decision. I think somehow she understands how we could have made such a terrible mistake.

Kristin, through the years, disproved all the dire predictions and advice of the physicians, nurses, and parents of children with disabilities. Oh, what she has done with her life—more than many people who have the correct number of chromosomes.

She started proving them wrong when she was an infant. Kristin was fascinated with the pictures we hung on the sides of her crib. As she grew, her curiosity increased and early on showed an amazing interest in learning which continues today. She seems to grab knowledge from so many sources, some very obscure. About a year ago she came out of her room and announced, "I had an epiphany." And then she told us what it was she had experienced. We asked her if she knew what epiphany meant and she told us the correct meaning. I asked where in the world she learned that word and she said, "Oh, they say it on *Friends*." (She watches the reruns of this television show.) She has an incredible vocabulary and it's growing. She has been a voracious reader for decades and usually spends time every day reading something on her Kindle.

Kristin has developed into a movie buff and is incredibly knowledgeable about current and classic films, directors, and actors and actresses.

Kristin writes on her computer every day. The book *People Who Need Help* which she talked about writing in 1987 never was written, but right now she is hard at work on a romance novel tentatively titled, *Crazy, Risky Love.* As of this date, Robert and I have not yet been given permission to read this book-in-progress, and to tell the truth, we're almost afraid to. Kristin has written all of the speeches she has given over the years. Either Robert or I sit at the computer and we type exactly what she says. Sometimes we will ask Kristin to clarify what she means and then she expands on her ideas. But, her presentations and Christmas newsletters are all her thoughts expressed in her own words.

Kristin has always loved the ocean. Lately, she likes to walk to the beach and write in her notebook. One of her essays is included at the end of her update to this book. It is called "The Sea."

From her early childhood on, independence has been important to Kristin. When she was young she was eager to get out and do things on her own, but Robert and I had fears and reservations. Robert was particularly protective of his little girl. She was tired of having her parents with her all of the time and had been asking to shop alone in the mall. Finally, one day she and Robert were sitting in the food court of a big shopping mall in Denver and Kristin again expressed her desire to shop alone. He finally consented. Later he told me how he "handled" her first excursion in the mall alone. Robert told me he watched as she walked out of the food court into the mall. He gave her a little time to get some distance, peeked around the corner to see where she was, and then he started to follow her. When she stopped to look at something, he quickly jumped into the entryway of the store nearest to him— again peeking around the corner to see where she was. This repeated—she would walk, he would creep along some distance behind her. She would stop and he would leap into an entry way and watch for her next move. This continued throughout her first "independent" trip exploring the mall. I told Robert he could have been arrested as a stalker.

Once, when she had just begun working at a large supermarket, she caught Robert and me with our noses pressed against the front window watching her work.

Kristin, though, has been able to work around her parents' worries and has proven herself able to live independently. In Denver she lived in her own apartment for over six years. She handles her own checking account, shops for her food, and cooks her own meals.

Near the end of the 1987 edition of *The Kristin Book* in the chapter titled "The Future," Robert speculates about what we may expect. He wrote, *"She'll not drive a car . . ."* Actually, she did, and probably could have gotten her license. When she was in her early 30's, she took driving lessons and passed the written test for her temporary permit. With a licensed driver in the car with her, she drove successfully around Denver many times. She also had several opportunities to drive on the interstate from Denver up to the mountains and back. I think, almost certainly, she could have passed the driving test to get her license, but she decided she didn't want to take a chance of hurting someone and told us she didn't want to get her license.

Robert also states in "The Future," *"... she'll not master the perplexing complexity of The Information age . . ."*

83

Kristin emails, texts, and uses the computer for her writing. I have several college degrees, but when I need to manipulate three remotes to get a DVD to play on our television, I have to call Kristin to do it for me. In all areas she has far exceeded everyone's expectations. Rarely does a week pass when she doesn't amaze us with new vocabulary, new ideas, new skills, and extraordinary insights about life and people.

Kristin has always been a "gutsy" little gal, from gladly "trying out" calamari and other squirmy marine cuisine to joyfully going out with us on a whale-watching trip on an extremely wild ocean. The only one in the boat who was not green-in-the-face was Kristin. She loves to get up in front of people and belt out karaoke songs, and she rode on a float in a parade in Newport, Oregon, dressed as a gigantic sea star. (I was a huge acorn barnacle on the float with Kristin.)

Many years ago, Robert, Kristin, and I were attending an afternoon Dixieland jazz concert at the Gerald R. Ford Amphitheater in Vail, Colorado. Much to my delight, I saw President Ford coming down the aisle near us, surrounded by serious-looking men in suits who looked like they really meant business. Much to my horror (and Robert's) we watched helplessly as Kristin quickly walked away from us heading for the President and his massive bodyguards. I had visions of machine guns and federal prison, but Kristin had visions of meeting a past President of the United States. And meet him she did. We watched as she slid in under the elbows of the stern-faced guards, held out her hand, and shook hands with the President. Robert and I were still in shock when she calmly walked back to where we sat frozen in our seats. I asked what she said and she told us, "I shook his hand and said, 'I am glad to meet you, President Ford.'" I have no idea how many years I aged in those few minutes.

Over the years Kristin has traveled extensively with Robert and me and now she travels with *Trips, Inc.* a company in Eugene, Oregon, that arranges tours around the world for people with disabilities. She talks about this in her part of this update to the original book.

I take great pride in her ability to be an active participant in the community. She is a strong advocate for herself and for all people with disabilities. In her part of this updated book she describes her advocacy activities. She has compassion and concern for the welfare of disabled people. I think this is wonderful.

Robert and I tried to ensure Kristin developed a strong self-concept. We always were extremely careful about the situations she was in and people she encountered. (When possible, we still try to keep an eye out for her.) We couldn't stop the crude comments and actions of junior high classmates and of some adults who were (and are) equally destructive, but she has always known how proud we are of her. Robert helped her every day before she met the public at her job at a supermarket in Denver. As she got out of the car he would give her part or all of the following advice, *"You have to forgive the fools every day. Give them your heart. Don't expect the world ever to be as nice as you are. They are lucky to have you."*

We have had many friends, relatives, and professional service providers who have been wonderful to Kristin and supportive to all three of us. They have invigorated and added richness to her life.

Do we have any fears? Yes. Robert and I worry about her life beyond our lives. We hope we have helped her build the skills and strengths she will need to live her life happily and safely without our support. We hope she will have some close friends to share her happiness. We hope she is not lonely, but involved, engaged, and busy as she is now.

How do I end this? Maybe I just wish for more of the same for many more years. Life with Kristin and Robert is wonderful. She's the best. She's loved. She's a gift to Robert and me.

Robert, Kristin, and I have given many presentations about Kristin's life with Down syndrome. Sometimes I would say to the audience that I once told Kristin, "If someone lined up all the daughters in the world and told me I could pick any one I wanted, I would pick you." I meant it then, and more than ever, I mean it now.

Introduction: Kristin's View

by

Robert Nichols

The view most of us have of the world is an approximation at best—a fiction contrived to create a story that supports biased beliefs and convenient omissions. This isn't just some home-brewed theory of yours truly. This is the stuff of mainstream brain science. It turns out that much of the comfort and security we feel about our lives is the product of selective perception.

To lead full and honest lives, we need to know a larger world than the one playing in the local movie house of our minds. This is where Kristin comes in as a voice with which the world needs to reckon.

Kristin described the disabled population of which she is a part as "people who need help." She planned to write a book by that title. It was going to tell the stories she knew in an attempt to help people understand her world. Well, she hasn't gotten around to finishing that work but she sure has done a great deal to further the acceptance and understanding of people who need help. As a self-advocacy activist, Kristin has given years to good causes and organizations aimed at securing people with disabilities their fair place in our society.

It's all about perception. When Kristin stands before an audience and says, "I want to tell you what it's like to be a person with Down syndrome," she establishes a direct link between what is real and what is approximated in the minds of the people who hear her words.

Following is a composite of several speeches Kristin has written and delivered to a variety of audiences about

the country at colleges, conferences, and once, inside the locked doors of a girl's detention center. This is the serious Kristin who fearlessly has stood before crowds of over a thousand people and spoken with an even and honest
voice, the difficult and wonderful essence of her life. (She's a short lady and at one event they had to find her a cinder block to stand on in order to see over the podium.) It is an important message she delivers. But, she's more fun to be around at home and when she is my traveling buddy full of giggles, wise cracks, and excitement for the moment. When she and Carol play UNO® card games at the kitchen table, it can get wild, believe me.

Kristin Speaks

by

Kristin Nichols

When I was born in 1970, the doctors said I wouldn't be able to do anything. The doctors didn't expect people with Down syndrome to do much with their lives. But the doctors were wrong.

There were many problems to face because I was born with Down syndrome. When I was little I had many health problems. I had a lot of colds and pneumonia. I also had heart problems. When I was three years old I had pneumonia and a high fever. After that I lost all my hair and now I wear a wig. Another problem was people would stare at me when I was a baby. It made my mom very upset when they stared at me.

There are some more bad things about having Down syndrome. Some people are cruel. When I was younger there were big problems I had to deal with. There were people who were very mean. In junior high there were kids who called me cruel names like "retard" and "retarded bitch." Some kids would spit on me when I got on the school bus. They used to pull off my wig. Later when I worked at Albertsons there were some people who disrespected me because I have Down syndrome. There was a person who looked at me and said, "You're a freak." As an adult, some people treat me like a child. So there are bad things in my life.

It is important to know, though, that most people are nice to me. I want to tell you about the wonderful things in my life.

You should know that I am living a great life. It turns out I can do many things like swim, make latch hook pillows and rugs, make mosaic glass art, play banjo, and dance. I take buses to go places on my own. In Denver I went to dances and parties with my friends.

For six years, when we lived in Denver I was in Magic Moments. Magic Moments is a theatrical musical group full of singing, dancing, and acting. I felt like a movie star up there on stage with such talented people, including people with disabilities. It was really magical, a dream come true.

In my spare time at home I love to read books and do crossword puzzles and I am writing a book—a romance novel about crazy and risky love. I also love to listen to music, dance, and watch movies and old TV shows. I like to play games and do exercise on my Wii. I love going to the mall and buying things like DVDs and CDs. Sometimes I walk by the ocean or kayak on a lake.

In Denver I spent a lot of time working. I had many different jobs. I was a courtesy clerk at a supermarket for over thirteen years.

Education is very important to me. Learning can be lots of fun and I learn a lot when I travel. My parents and I have been to many places in Oregon. I rode a camel at Wildlife Safari and went on a jet boat ride on the Rogue River. I went on an ocean marine boat tour where I got to hold a Dungeness crab.

I'm an international, world traveler. My parents and I have been to England, Scotland, Italy, France, Switzerland, Mexico, the Caribbean, Brazil, Peru, Roatan, British Columbia, Canada, and all over the United States. I snorkeled in the Caribbean and in Honduras. I swam with stingrays and dolphins. I kayaked down a jungle river in Belize. We stayed in the Amazon Rainforest. We travelled to Lima, Peru, and then explored Machu Picchu.

Now I am also traveling with *Trips, Inc.* which is a company in Eugene, Oregon, that arranges trips for people with disabilities. With *Trips, Inc.* I have been to Hawaii, Alaska, the Greek Islands, the Caribbean, to the Pendleton Oregon Rodeo Roundup, and I will be going to Scandinavia and Russia.

I learn a lot when I travel. I have learned about many places and met many people. What is so interesting about different cultures is that you learn a lot from different people. You can learn about their language, about the kind of music they are into, and learn about different holidays.

I have always loved making decisions and doing things on my own. Since I was a little girl I wanted to go places by myself. At the age of five I ditched preschool and decided to take a walk. The teacher finally found me at a bowling alley. My mom and dad wanted me to be independent and face life on my own, but not so soon.

For over six years in Denver I lived alone in my own apartment.

I like to be independent. I do things on my own. My mother and father want me to make my own decisions. If there is a big decision that I have to make, I talk it over with my mom and dad to get their opinion. They usually have great judgment and it helps me to talk with them. Then I tell them, "I'll take it under advisement." This drives them crazy. But they trust what I do.

I think it is important for disabled people to get into the community. We need to let the community know we are here and that we can be a very important part of the community. We want them to know we are valuable human beings with feelings. This isn't easy. People can be very mean, say hurtful things, and stare. When this happens I try to treat the person with understanding. I think they say these hurtful things because I am different from them and they don't understand and they are afraid. I try to be patient with them and let them see that I am a person with human feelings and I am not someone to be afraid of. I try to do things to make them feel comfortable with me. When they are comfortable with me, sometimes they aren't afraid of my differences and they treat me better.

I know when I go out into the world people can be hateful. But if I just stayed home, I would miss learning things in that world. I go out because the world is out there and I have a right to be a part of the world. I have Down syndrome, but I also have abilities, talents, and skills. If people think of me only as a person with a disability, they are just seeing the disability which is only one little part of me. They are missing all the rest of me. They are not seeing how valuable I can be.

In the community I live in now, I take tai chi classes, exercise at a gym, and I've taken classes in yoga, mosaics, and acrylic painting. I volunteer in the library once a week.

I have helped people with disabilities. In Denver, when I was eighteen I started speaking to groups of teachers, parent groups, high school students, students in graduate classes at University of Denver, and doctors. In Oregon I have spoken at conferences and at two Buddy Walks.

I tell them what it's like to have a disability and what people with disabilities need. I have also been on boards of directors in Colorado and in Oregon. For two years I was a member of the Board of Directors of the National Down Syndrome Congress.

In 2010 and 2011, I helped people with disabilities in Oregon. I had a year of training. I listened to speakers, toured the Capitol in Salem. We learned how to get into the community to meet new people. We did role playing on how to interview. Then we did one-to-one interviews with teachers, with people involved in disability services, and with a person in the Oregon government—like a senator. The point of these interviews was to help us make connections in our communities and in the state. These are people we can call when we are trying to help make changes. We learned that all people, including people with disabilities, have the right to testify at local and state hearings. We learned how to testify to senate subcommittees.

On March 17, 2011, I testified to a real Oregon State Senate subcommittee about a bill that would take the word "retarded" out of public school papers. The bill passed.

I also was invited to sit on the floor of the Oregon State Senate with Senator Joanne Verger and she introduced me to the senate members.

I am a real good friend to my parents. They are very happy and proud of me. My mom and dad like my life I'm living now.

I really love my life. This is the life I always wanted and I got it.

There are a lot of people who have disabilities. They are learning things in their world like learning how to get along in their lives and learning how to be proud of who they are and what they have. They need to be happy about who they are no matter what their disability is.

If you know people with disabilities, don't be sad, because their lives can be wonderful just like mine. They should know about the world, they should know how to be independent, they should know how to be happy, and they should know how to feel proud of themselves.

My Passions

by

Kristin Nichols

I want to tell you about my passions in life. About the things that make me feel great about myself.

Music. The reason I love music so much is because it comes through my heart. It carries the vibrations that make me feel like dancing in the air, like I'm flying with the stars. There is a different kind of music I know—the music I hear from the ocean waves while I dance on the sandy beach. It feels like the waves are dancing with me. I was born to love music. It feels magical to me.

Movies. When I watch movies I get into the characters played by the actors and actresses. I feel like I'm there with them. I feel their passion, their pain, their love. I feel their hearts. Movies inspire me.

Dancing. Dancing makes me feel very happy. I feel a tingle like laughter when I get into movements and the beat and the meaning of the words of songs. But, also, when I dance, I feel a mood of movement that makes the music flow to my heart like a red rose blooms, but it shines like a rainbow and it feels like I am the storm that makes the music. I feel like I'm in a different universe when I dance.

TV. I've been watching television all my life. Captain Kangaroo was my friend when I was little. My first favorite Muppet was Kermit the Frog. I loved The Count, Cookie Monster, and Oscar the Grouch, too. When I was older, I started watching crime drama. At the International Special Olympics in 1988, I did my gymnastics floor routine to the theme music of *Miami Vice.* Sonny Crockett is my favorite even today. I love Don Johnson. In the 90s I loved to watch *Friends.* I felt like I was one of them, like when they

94

were having coffee and conversation I was there with them. Television is educational to me. It teaches me about the world.

My life. Every morning when I wake up, I say good morning to my Universe and my Inner Universe. I drum my spirit drum and then I start my day. Every day is a magical mystery. I don't know what I'm going to do that day, but I always try to make it fun, no matter what I do. I give my heart of passion to every day.

I love to walk to the beach and spend time writing. This is my essay titled, *The Sea.*

March 31, 2013

The Sea

By

Kristin Nichols

When I'm walking on the sandy beach I feel like I'm walking on air of freedom. When I can hear and feel the waves singing and talking to me like an old friend, they are saying, *Let me talk and sing to you so you can dance up to the sky. The musical waves will be touching you with love and passion. Feel the wind of the waves dancing with you. Let me take you flying in the shadow of the night air. Follow your heart, listen to the musical waves and dancing stars. Let me take you away to the one you love deeply waiting for you. I love the way you are here with me. I'll make sure you are happy. I love the way you dance with me, my friend.*

I can feel the compassion for me from the waves. I feel the love from the sea and the sea loves me.

The way I dance I feel like walking on the sandy beach with my bare feet flying with the stars at night. It feels like a tickle. It makes me feel magical inside my deep heart. It makes me feel like laughing.

When I dream of the sea I can hear the waves calling me saying, *Kristin, come to me. I want to talk to you.* The sea knows my name.

I am awake and I rise from my bed. I get dressed and I start to walk to the beach in the middle of the night. I was listening to the waves. They said to me, "*I have something for you. Come with me. I will take you somewhere. Fly with me in the stars of the sky. Close your eyes and feel the night air.* I am saying to the sea, "I'm flying! I feel something inside me that makes me warm. What is it?" I ask the waves and the stars of the night. Both of them say to me, "*You are here, Kristin. Feel the heart of love from someone who loves you. Open your eyes. There is a man on the beach standing there looking at an angel flying toward him.*"

I open my eyes. I am falling from the sky and a man sees me falling. He catches me in his arms and saves me. The man asks, "Are you an angel? Let me look at you. Let me see you." He touches my chin lightly. I look at him and he looks at me and smiles at me. He asks me to dance with him and I say, "Yes." We dance with the ocean waves and feel the heart of passion and love. The man says, "You are my angel of the stars and you are my love. You are my star of the sea. Come with me and learn life with me."

The way I feel about love comes from the sea. The sea tells me, "Don't worry about finding someone. Just feel the freedom. Enjoy life."

Relevance?

by

Robert Nichols

So, again, what is the relevance today of a forty-year old story?

And, of course, what does this forty-plus-year-old tale of one small family's challenges and joys have to do with the state of the Twenty-First Century?

Unfortunately, plenty. What Carol and I encountered in 1970 with the birth of our child with a chromosomal abnormality, Down syndrome, was an abysmal lack of understanding, sensitivity, and useful support. Some would contend that the decades hence have corrected much of this with advances in science, awareness, and information. I mean, if we just could have Googled *Mongolism* that sad day in the hospital when the best source we had was medical people who were bombarding us with terms like "vegetable" and "hopeless," we could have saved ourselves a world of hurt. Right?

Perhaps. But, of course, there is much more to this story than the wisdom of Wikipedia in its most recent refinement could address. In some more subtle ways, Kristin's story is as relevant this March afternoon in 2013 as it was during the early years of her life. When Carol and I talk to young parents of children with disabilities we have found the Information Age has done little to allay the emotional and social aspects of this difficult situation. I mean, true, we have replaced the words "handicapped" and 'retarded' with 'developmentally delayed' or "disabled." Our language is more careful, our policies more cognizant of attitude and affect. Kristin testified at the state Capitol at a senate hearing in support of a proposed law that would take the word 'retarded' out of any official documents. This is all great, but hardly enough.

Much so-called progress in our times is political correctness rather than cultural evolution. There are considerably fewer folks who throw the word 'retard' around, but there are plenty who speak 'correctly' but perceive with ignorance. Some years ago, a prominent politician discussing funding for special needs programs said, "We spend $20,000 dollars educating *these people* and all they can do is roll over in a bed." The head of the bio-ethics department of a large Eastern university has openly advocated euthanizing all infants born with Down syndrome. This fellow, along with such renowned humanitarians as Adolph Hitler, would have gassed my baby before she had a chance to bless this world with her first smile.

This story is relevant to this day. The more that you know about my daughter, the better you will be prepared to treat her and her many peers in our society with compassion, fairness, and respect. I hope that Kristin's story will encourage kind treatment of all people, regardless of disability, who deserve acceptance and support in this world.

And, at a more basic level, the relevance of Kristin's story has little to do with the circumstances of her condition, and much to do with the ever-contemporary challenge of a family confronting difficulty with love, humor, and compassion.

Carol and Kristin's annual
Christmas cookie
and Wilson Picket
celebration, 2002

Music

Kristin takes a bow:
Magic Moments,
2001

Machu Pichu, Peru
2003

Mosaic art.
Kristin and
her mosaic
butterfly at
community
art show.

101

Kristin Snorkeling, Cozumel

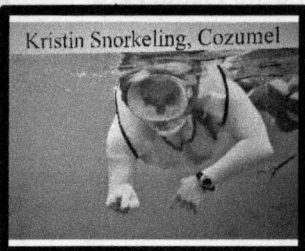

Kristin on
and in the water.

Other Works by Robert Nichols

Most of these titles are currently published as e-Books available through all the major distributors—Kindle, Nook, etc.

Also, printed editions are in process as books-on-demand, I will get them out—hey, it's a lot of work.

Books etc.

The Kristin Book (1987)

Story of the first fifteen years of the life of my daughter who was born with Down Syndrome.

This book, reissued with an update, is now available in eBook format as ***The Kristin Book: Update 2013***

Take the Aspen Train (1988)

Co-authored with Edward Larsh. Coffee table, Colorado history / social philosophy / train book. *(No longer available.)*

Adventures in the High Wind (1990)

Collection of my poems, stories, and essays.
eBook edition, 2013.

Leadville, U.S.A (1993)

Co-authored with Edward Larsh. Oral history of Leadville, Colorado. *(No longer available.)*

The High Priest of Hallelujah (1999)

Niche-less novel of poetic vision, humor, and satire.
eBook edition, 2015.

Summer Words, 2000 (2001)

Collection of short essays about laughter, God, knife throwing and much more.
e-Book edition, 2014.

The Booklets (2001 and...)

12-14 page booklets of poetry, short stories, essays—you know: literature. Currently there are five of these little gems published with more to come. Some day...

The Five Great Truths of Uncle Bob (2002)

A culminating work of philosophy, religion, and practical wisdom (and all on one side of a sheet of paper).

God of the Poets (2003)

It took me twenty years to get this one right. When I finished the first version in '83 I didn't know enough to write my own novel. Perhaps now I do. I was pretty much just a stenographer for the real author, God. This isn't traditional stuff. It's a story of art, love, humanity and... *the purpose of life*.
e-Book edition, 2014.

Albatross: The Curse of Honesty (2013)

The first novel I wrote, and re-wrote, and finally published. It's a funny and touching tale of a fellow whose life is nearly destoyed by the curse of absolute honesty.

The Great Book of Bob (2009)
The Great Book of Bob **eBook edition** (2014)

A unified collection of humorous, soul-wrenching, and harshly honest tales and thoughts gleaned from a lifelong love story—
stories of a poet's love of sunrises, poetic epiphanies, laughter, and for the soulmate of his life. And the best part about it, it's not some icky-sticky, lovey-poo bunch of hearts and flowers. It's hard-edged wonder and real reason for all of us to be glad to be alive. I tell *my* stories that we may each realize the significance of our own.

Uncle Bob's Big Book of Happy (2017)

I should make this clear from the start. None of this is easy. The first chapter of this work starts out saying exactly that: This will not be easy. I tell some hard truths. Don't be misled by the mirthful lilt of my title. Uncle Bob here will do his best to help you be happy, but none of this means diddly-squat if you can't face harsher aspects of our everyday journey. I write this book in hopes that my stories, theories, blathering bilge and sublime prayers may be of help to you in avoiding the burden, the curse of bitterness. It's no fun living in a world of bitchy whiners, angry jerks, and cranky bastards. You know what I mean.

THE FOOTLOCKER SERIES

This is a series of eBooks gleaned from fifty years of writing excavated from Robert Nichols' old footlocker of notebooks and scraps of papers—the repository of a life of art.

For information contact Robert Nichols at Mtmuse44@aol.com.

Titles:

about Time
about Mountain Living
about Seasons
about Paths

about Time: Poems and Other Stories (2015)

The first in the series—poetry, stories, and photography about ancient time, the time of children, the time of young adults, and the time of growing old. It's really not about time at all. This is a book about life.

about Mountain Living: Finding a Way (2015)

A journey told in story and poem. A life trek from discontent and restlessness to commitment and discovery. This work tells of a succession of habitats and lifestyles progressing farther and farther from the city and further into a better destiny—from apartment to cabin to tipi to hilltop shrine of art, nature, and spirit. A journey from complacent certainty to out-on-the-edge primal survival. Perhaps my story will encourage yours. And, beyond the tale I tell, just read the poems and stories as the art they are intended to be. You will laugh and weep and contemplate—you will be changed.

about Seasons: the Wind and Weather of Our Days (2016)

Poems of the seasons—not just some cliché sweetness about leaves and blossoms either. This is the core stuff of being. Seasons, wind, and weather—the fierce and beautiful power of Nature that can keep us humble and exhilarated throughout our lives. It is the very "life and death" intensity of these metamorphic cycles that excites the turning of our years with risk and wonder. Time takes away our days, storms wash away our safety, seasons etch our flesh with danger. Old Spirits out on the plains once told me, "Earth shall never be tame... celebrate your fear and feel you are alive!" Yes!

about Paths—Journeys Through Wonder, Danger, and Self

The fourth in the Footlocker Series of books published by Robert Nichols, about Paths is another collection of beautiful and moving poetry and thought-provoking essays. Robert artfully takes you with him as he recounts youthful journeys hitchhiking the country, expresses vignette word-sketches of people and places along the way throughout the years, and gives a sense of purpose to the paths all of us take. Read these works and you will know the harsh and enlightening truths of the road, you will contemplate the ugly realities of American racism, you will observe the humor and pathos of the passing scene—you will travel the path of an open-hearted poet.

Robert Nichols writes, carves, sings,
and loves life with his family in Oregon.
(This photo was taken at Wildlife Safari in Oregon.
Our homely friend is Frank, the Camel.)

www.ingramcontent.com/pod-product-compliance
Lightning Source LLC
Chambersburg PA
CBHW072040040426

42447CB00012BB/2950